UNTO US A
SON
IS GIVEN

KYREN J. GAREL

UNTO US A SON IS GIVEN

THE TRANSFORMATIVE POWER OF SONSHIP

KEEN VISION PUBLISHING

Printed in the United States of America
Keen Vision Publishing, LLC
www.publishwithkvp.com
ISBN: 979-8-9912210-6-1

For every son.
It's time to take your seat.

JOIN THE COMMUNITY

Scan the QR code to connect with King's Academy, an exclusive community on Mighty Networks designed to empower, equip, and walk with you on your journey of sonship. Dive deeper into transformational teachings, engage in meaningful conversations, and grow alongside others embracing their divine identity. Your seat in the family is waiting—let's walk this path together!

CONTENTS

FOREWORD

In the heart of the Christian faith lies a profound truth that many believers yearn to understand more deeply: the concept of sonship. As children of God, we are invited into a relationship that transcends mere obedience or servitude. It is a call to embrace our identity as sons and daughters of the Almighty and to walk in the love, inheritance, and authority that comes with this divine adoption.

This book, which you now hold in your possession, is more than a theological treatise or a collection of inspirational thoughts. It is a journey. A journey into the very essence of what it means to be a son or daughter of God. In a world that often leaves us questioning our worth and purpose, understanding our identity in Christ as beloved children is crucial. It is through this lens that we find our true value, our eternal purpose, and the deep love that God has for each of us.

Kyren Garel, the author of this book, has brought a unique perspective to the concept of sonship. His approach, which combines biblical insight, personal experience, and practical wisdom, is a refreshing take on a fundamental aspect of the Christian faith. Whether you are a seasoned believer or new to the faith, this book will challenge you to rethink how you see yourself in relation to God. It will encourage you to step into the fullness of your inheritance as a child of God, to live out the privileges and responsibilities that come with sonship, and to walk confidently in your divine identity.

Kyren is God's son, Kyren is his mother's son, and Kyren is my spiritual son. He understands the posture of sonship. For seven years, I have watched him embrace every facet of being a son and thus benefit from every facet of being a son. Sonship covers, sonship protects, sonship instructs, and sonship corrects. Something else that sonship does is announce. I announce that this is the inaugural literary work of one that will continually provide guidance to this generation regarding how to fully maximize their God-given life. Kyren Garel is a voice that can be trusted.

As you embark on this transformative journey, I encourage you to open your heart and mind to the truths that are shared. Let the words within these pages draw you closer to the Father, deepen your relationship with Him, and empower you to live as a true son or daughter of the King. May this book be a powerful tool in your spiritual growth and a constant reminder of the boundless love and grace our Heavenly Father has lavished upon us all. Welcome to Sonship!

In Christ,
Dr. Khaalida T. Forbes

SERVING IS NOT JUST AN ACT OF HUMIILTY…

IT IS A PATHWAY TO DESTINY.

INTRODUCTION

In a world where the concept of sonship often gets lost in the noise of daily struggles and is overshadowed by contemporary narratives, it is essential to rediscover what it truly means to be a son in the biblical sense. My journey, though unique in its trajectory, reflects a universal quest for identity and purpose. Growing up in Grand Rapids, Michigan, under the nurturing care of my mother, Lucinda Garel, and in the absence of my biological father, I experienced firsthand how the concept of sonship was not just a theological query but a lived reality, shaping my understanding of self and my relationship with God.

In the grand narrative of human history, there are moments when the divine intersects with the mundane in profound ways. The birth of Jesus Christ, as told in the scriptures, is the epitome of such a moment—a time when God intervened directly in human history, setting in motion a story of redemption and transformation. This book, *Unto Us a Son Is Given*, aims to explore this divine intersection, not only as it pertains to Christ but also as a reflection of our own lives and destinies.

Your birth marks a specific moment in time when God decided to intervene directly with the history of humanity. Like Christ, each person is born into this world with a divine purpose, intricately woven into the larger tapestry of God's plan. This book delves into the depths of what it means to be a son in the biblical sense, exploring how this ancient concept is still profoundly relevant today.

The phrase *"For unto us a child is born, unto us a son is given"* encapsulates a dual truth. The historical and spiritual narrative of Jesus speaks of the miraculous intersection of humanity and divinity - the birth of a child and the giving of a Son. This theological framework provides a lens through which we can view our own existence. Each of us, in being born, has been brought into this world by divine will, and in being given, we find our purpose within God's overarching story.

This book invites you to explore the essence of sonship. It's an exploration that transcends mere academic pursuit; it's about delving into a living, breathing reality that defines our identity, purpose, and divine relationship. Sonship in the Christian context extends far beyond a title or familial bond—it is a journey of faith, a calling of obedience, and a promise of inheritance that transcends the physical realm. As we embark on this journey, we will delve into the historical and cultural nuances of sonship as understood in biblical times, contrasting them with our contemporary perspectives. This exploration is crucial for understanding how the biblical portrayal of sonship, especially as exemplified by Jesus Christ, the Son of God, reshapes our understanding of ourselves as children of God.

In my life, from the mentors who filled the void left by my father to my spiritual development under the guidance of my pastors at Truth City Church, I have witnessed how God intricately crafts our understanding of sonship. This book is a reflection of that journey—an exploration of how the biblical concept of sonship transcends time, culture, and personal circumstances to speak into the heart of every individual.

Through the scriptures, historical context, and personal anecdotes, this book aims to illuminate the concept of sonship in a way that resonates with your story. We will explore various facets of sonship, including submission, obedience, adoption, and inheritance. We'll unravel the complexities of birthrights, divine commission, and the responsibilities that come with being a son of God. Moreover, we will address the challenges faced in this journey, both internally in our spiritual walk and externally in our interaction with the world.

A pivotal focus of this book is the service aspect of sonship. Serving is not just an act of humility; it is a pathway to destiny, a foundational element in the journey of a son. Through service, we align ourselves with God's purpose, nurturing our spiritual growth and advancing the Kingdom of God. This book also aims to dispel myths and misconceptions about sonship, aligning our understanding with biblical truths. We will draw upon scriptural references, historical contexts, and practical examples to paint a comprehensive picture of what it means to live in the posture of a son.

Unto Us a Son Is Given is an invitation to explore and embrace the call to sonship. It is my hope that these pages will inspire, challenge, and equip you to step into the fullness of what it means to be a son in the Kingdom of God. Welcome to a journey of discovery, transformation, and fulfillment. Welcome to the exploration of your divine destiny as a son.

$\mathscr{S}$ONSHIP?

Whenen we think about being a son, our minds often jump to our families, right? But in this chapter, we will explore a deeper, more profound kind of sonship—the kind that's talked about in the Bible. It's a concept loaded with meaning, history, and some serious power for how we live our lives today.

In ancient cultures, sonship was all about your place in the family and society. If you were the firstborn, you were pretty much the VIP – set to inherit not just your dad's land or business but also his social status and responsibilities. But here's the twist: when we look at this idea through the lens of Christianity, it takes on a whole new dimension. We're not just talking about family trees here; we're talking about a spiritual family that crosses all sorts of borders and boundaries.

Think about it this way: In Christianity, being a son of God is kind of like being invited into a royal family. It's about more than just being born into it; it's about being chosen and adopted into this divine lineage. This concept flips the script on what it traditionally meant to be a son. Instead of just inheriting what's been passed down, it's about stepping into a whole new identity. So, why should we care about this ancient concept today? Good question. Understanding biblical sonship changes how we see ourselves in the grand scheme of things. It's not just about where we come from; it's about where we're heading. It's about finding a sense of belonging and purpose beyond our immediate family or cultural background.

Growing up without my biological father around, the idea of sonship felt a bit abstract to me. It was like there was this club that I wasn't a part of. But as I started to explore what sonship meant in the Bible, I realized it was about something much bigger and more inclusive. It was like getting invited to a family I didn't even know I was missing.

In the Bible, sonship is about being part of God's family, and this family is open to everyone – no exclusions. It's about being connected to something timeless, something eternal. This kind of sonship offers us a new way to look at our lives, our relationships, and the world around us. It's about being part of a story that's way bigger than just our own.

I invite you to open your mind and heart to this idea as we unpack the concept of sonship. Whether you've known your parents all your life or have walked a path similar to mine, there's something in this journey for everyone. It's about discovering a connection to a divine family that brings with it a sense of identity, purpose, and belonging. So, are you ready to dive into this adventure and discover what sonship really means? Let's go!

This idea of sonship transcends cultural, ethnic, and even temporal boundaries. It's a universal concept, inviting all individuals, regardless of their backgrounds or life stories, to be part of a grander narrative. It's about being acknowledged and embraced not just for who we are but for who we can become. This spiritual kinship offers us a place in a family that is boundless, unconditional, and enduring.

In a world where identity and belonging are often questioned, this concept of sonship provides a reassuring answer. It tells us that our worth is not dependent on our earthly achievements or failures but on our inherent value as members of this divine family. It's a message of hope and empowerment, reminding us that we are more than the sum of our experiences. Moreover, understanding sonship in this context opens up new avenues for how we interact with others. It teaches us about love, acceptance, and forgiveness. As sons in this spiritual sense, we learn to see others not as strangers but as fellow members of this vast family. This perspective encourages compassion, empathy, and a deeper understanding of the human experience.

The journey to understand and embrace this concept of sonship is both personal and collective. It's personal because it requires us to reflect on our beliefs, our values, and our understanding of our place in the world. It's a path that might challenge our preconceived notions and push us to grow in ways we never expected. Yet, it's also a collective journey because it connects us with a community of believers who support, nurture, and enrich our understanding of this concept. As we delve deeper into the biblical teachings about sonship, we'll discover its profound implications for our spiritual growth. We'll explore how this identity shapes our relationship with God, ourselves, and the world. We'll examine the responsibilities that come with this role and how it empowers us to live lives of purpose and meaning.

This exploration of sonship is not just an academic exercise; it's a transformative experience. It's about opening our hearts to a deeper understanding of love, acceptance, and belonging. It's about finding comfort in knowing we are part of something much larger than ourselves. It's an invitation to experience the joy and peace that comes from this spiritual connection. Throughout this journey, I encourage you to ask questions, seek answers, and be open to the insights this exploration will bring. It's a path that may lead to unexpected discoveries and profound realizations. It's a journey that promises to enrich your life and deepen your faith.

So, together, let's approach this journey with curiosity, openness, and a willingness to embrace the unknown. Let's explore the depths of what it means to be a son in the broadest, most inclusive sense of the term. Together, let's uncover the beauty, wisdom, and power of this ancient yet ever-relevant concept of sonship.

MY PATH TO UNDERSTANDING SONSHIP

My path to understanding sonship was not straightforward; it resembled a winding road with its fair share of bumps and turns. While growing up, the world around me largely influenced my perception of what it meant to be a son. I saw families with fathers who were present, actively involved, and guiding their children. However, my own experience was quite different. My biological father was not a part of my life, which left a significant void and raised a crucial question in my mind: What does it truly mean to be a son?

For a long time, I grappled with this absence, feeling like there was a missing piece in the puzzle of my identity. In my quest for answers, I turned to various sources – friends, mentors, and even fictional characters from books and movies. Each provided a fragment of understanding, but the overall picture of sonship remained incomplete. It felt like I was trying to understand and fulfill a role I had no script for. The significant turning point in my journey came when I began to delve deeper into my faith. In the Bible, I found references to God as a Father, but this was unlike any father figure I had previously encountered. Here was a Father characterized by perpetual presence, boundless care, and unconditional love. This revelation marked a radical shift from my previous understanding of sonship. The notion of being spiritually adopted by

God was astonishing. It was not about replacing my earthly father or rewriting my past but rather about embracing a new identity that had always been available to me, yet I had not fully grasped it. I realized I was being invited into a divine family, and this realization changed everything for me.

Understanding myself as a son of God has profoundly transformed my entire outlook on life – my sense of self-worth, my purpose, and the nature of my relationships. It's akin to walking into a room where I had always felt out of place, only to discover that it was actually designed with me in mind. I was no longer just a boy without a dad; I had become a child of the King, part of a grander narrative, with a unique role that only I could fulfill.

I hope to connect with your experiences by sharing this part of my journey. Perhaps you have felt a similar emptiness or have wrestled with comparable questions about your identity. Your experience and understanding of sonship might differ from mine, and that is the beauty of this journey – it is as unique as each individual who embarks upon it. I invite you to join me in exploring what it means to be a son in a spiritual sense. This journey is not limited by your background, the struggles you have faced, or the doubts you may harbor. There is a place for you in this story, a story that is rich with meaning and beauty. Trust me, it's a journey worth undertaking.

This path to understanding sonship is a journey of self-discovery and spiritual growth. It's about uncovering layers of meaning and connecting with a concept that is both ancient and profoundly relevant. As we walk this path together, we open ourselves to new perspectives, allowing us to see beyond our immediate circumstances and into a world of deeper spiritual connections. It's about recognizing that we are part of something much larger than ourselves – a divine narrative that spans across time and space.

On this journey together, I encourage you to reflect on your own experiences and beliefs. This exploration is not just about understanding a concept; it's about experiencing a transformation. It's about finding a sense of belonging and purpose that transcends the physical and taps into the spiritual. Together, let's explore the depths of what it means to be a part of this divine family, to understand our place in it, and to embrace the roles we are meant to play. This journey is not without its challenges, but it is filled with moments of profound realization and growth. It's an opportunity to look within and around and understand our connections with the divine and each other. It's a chance to see ourselves and the world through a lens of spiritual sonship and grasp the responsibilities and joys that come with it.

So, as we embark on this exploration, let's do so with open hearts and minds. Let's be willing to question, to learn, and to grow. No matter where you are on this path, whether you are just beginning or have been on it for some time, know that this journey of understanding sonship is continuous, offering insights and revelations at every turn. It's a beautiful, enriching journey, and I am delighted to share it with you. Let's discover together the fullness and richness of what it means to be sons in the truest, most spiritual sense.

SONSHIP IN SCRIPTURE

When we delve into the Bible, the concept of sonship emerges not merely as a term but as a profound theme intricately woven into the fabric of Scripture, from Genesis to Revelation. This theme of sonship is a golden thread that offers us vital insights into our place within God's grand narrative. In the Old Testament, sonship is framed within specific contexts. It revolves around lineage, inheritance, and the fulfillment of divine promises. Consider the stories of patriarchs like Abraham, Isaac, and Jacob, whose lives were fundamentally about perpetuating God's work across generations. Moreover, the nation of Israel was collectively referred to as God's "son," signifying a unique and covenantal relationship with the divine.

The narrative takes a compelling turn with the advent of the New Testament. The arrival of Jesus Christ revolutionizes the concept of sonship. No longer is it confined to the boundaries of biological lineage or ethnicity. Instead, it transcends into the realm of spiritual rebirth and belonging. Jesus, as the quintessential Son, exemplifies a new paradigm of relationship with God – one that is intimate, loving, and inclusively accessible to all, irrespective of their backgrounds.

This is where the narrative becomes exhilarating. The apostle Paul, particularly in his letters to the Romans and Galatians, dramatically expands the scope of sonship. He articulates that sonship is no longer restricted by ethnicity, gender, or social status. Faith in Jesus Christ ushers individuals into this extraordinary spiritual family, with God Himself as the Father. This is not merely a comforting message; it represents a fundamental transformation in identity and inheritance. As sons in this spiritual context, we are not merely awaiting spiritual rewards in the afterlife. Instead, we are called to actively live out this identity in the present. We become heirs to a kingdom, entrusted with responsibilities and blessings that commence the moment we embrace this familial bond.

The depiction of sonship in the Bible centers around a relationship that is deeply personal and accessible. It's a relationship where individuals can approach God with their fears, aspirations, and shortcomings, secure in the knowledge that they are heard, loved, and valued. Understanding sonship from a biblical perspective has far-reaching implications for how we interact with God and conduct our lives. It shifts our understanding from seeing ourselves merely as creations of God to recognizing ourselves as children of God. This transformative realization influences how we perceive ourselves and our role in the world.

This biblical sonship is about more than just a title or a theological concept; it's about a living, breathing relationship with the divine. It's about realizing that our identity as God's children is not static but dynamic, evolving as we grow in our faith and understanding. This relationship invites us to participate actively in God's work, to be co-creators in His kingdom here on Earth. Moreover, this understanding of sonship has profound implications for how we view others. It encourages us to see every individual as a potential brother or sister in this expansive spiritual family. It fosters a sense of unity and purpose that transcends cultural, racial, and social barriers. This perspective of sonship nurtures a sense of belonging and community that is vital in a world often marked by division and isolation.

While exploring this theme further, we come to realize that sonship is not merely about privileges; it's also about responsibilities. As children of God, we are called to embody His values and teachings, to be lights in a world that often dwells in darkness. This calling is both a privilege and a responsibility, one that challenges us to live lives that reflect our divine heritage. In essence, the biblical concept of sonship is a journey of discovery, relationship, and transformation. It invites us into a deeper, more meaningful relationship with God, one where we are continuously learning, growing, and being shaped into His likeness. It's a journey that is as challenging as it is rewarding, offering us a new lens through which to view ourselves and the world around us. So, why should we care about this biblical perspective of sonship? Because it offers us a new identity, a new purpose, and a new way of living. It transforms our understanding of who we are and what we are called to be. It's a powerful truth that has the potential to revolutionize our lives, reshaping how we interact with God, with ourselves, and with the world around us. This understanding of sonship is a gift, a calling, and a journey all rolled into one, and it is a journey well worth taking.

SONSHIP TODAY

Here we are, inhabiting a world that is markedly different from the times depicted in the Bible. Yet, the ancient concept of sonship retains an astounding relevance in our contemporary lives. Far from being a relic of the past, sonship is a vibrant and living truth, profoundly influencing how we navigate our existence today. In the context of our modern world, sonship transcends mere titles or statuses; it embodies a way of life that molds our interactions, guides our decision-making, and shapes our self-perception. It involves embodying the knowledge of being part of God's family in every facet of our daily existence, living with a sense of purpose and confidence derived from the realization that we are loved and chosen by the Creator.

Recalling our sonship can provide immense strength and solace in times of doubt or adversity. It serves as a powerful reminder that we are not isolated in our struggles; we have a Heavenly Father deeply involved in our lives, sharing in our joys and sorrows. In a society where identity and belonging are often elusive, understanding our sonship offers a firm foundation and a sense of unshakeable identity.

In today's world, rife with divisions along cultural, social, and religious lines, the Christian concept of sonship acts as a unifying force. It transcends these divides, affirming that there is no place for prejudice or exclusion in God's family. We stand as equals, uniformly cherished, and called to embrace and live out this collective identity. Embracing our identity as children of God transcends self-assurance; it is about being equipped to enact change, act compassionately, and be conduits of God's love in the world. It's a clarion call to action, urging us to embody Kingdom values in our communities and beyond. This understanding of sonship challenges us to not just bask in the comfort of being loved by God but to actively extend that love to others, to live in a way that reflects the grace, truth, and love of our Heavenly Father.

After much reflection, I hope you begin to perceive sonship in a renewed light. It is more than a biblical concept; it's a tangible reality that can revolutionize how you live, think, and interact with those around you. Remember, being a child of God isn't solely about the privileges it brings; it's predominantly about how you utilize this identity. It's about leading a life that mirrors the virtues and teachings of our Heavenly Father.

Turning the page to the next chapter, we will delve deeper into one of the most profound elements of sonship:

adoption. We will explore the significance of being spiritually adopted into God's family. This exploration will cover the incredible transformation that spiritual adoption brings and how it reshapes our entire perception of our identity. This journey into understanding spiritual adoption is not just about acknowledging a theological concept; it's about experiencing a fundamental change in how we view ourselves and our place in the world. It's about recognizing that our relationship with God is not defined by mere creation but is deepened by the powerful act of being chosen and accepted as His own. This understanding brings a profound sense of belonging, purpose, and a new way of experiencing life.

So, as we embark on this exploration of spiritual adoption, prepare to uncover the depths of what it means to be a part of God's family. We will delve into how this new identity affects our relationships, our sense of self, and our role in the broader narrative of life. It's a journey that promises to be enlightening, transformative, and deeply enriching, offering a new perspective on what it truly means to be a child of God.

"YOU ARE NOW PART OF MY FAMILY. YOU BELONG WITH ME."

-GOD

CHAPTER TWO

ADOPTION: A SON'S JOURNEY

This chapter explores one of our faith journey's most heartwarming and powerful aspects—spiritual adoption. This isn't your typical adoption story; it's about being welcomed into an eternal, divine family. And trust me, it's a game-changer.

WHAT DOES SPIRITUAL ADOPTION MEAN?

Let's delve deeper and break down the concept of spiritual adoption, which transcends the physical world's understanding of adoption. In the physical sense, adoption means a child is chosen to become part of a new family, assuming a new role within that familial structure. However, in the spiritual realm, the concept of adoption takes on a profoundly deeper significance. When God adopts us, it is not merely about giving us a new family name; it is about bestowing upon us an entirely new identity. We transition from being mere believers or followers to becoming sons of the Most High. This new title comes laden with profound love, acceptance, and responsibility.

Imagine the act of hitting the refresh button on your life. That's the essence of what spiritual adoption embodies. It signifies a new beginning, a rebirth of sorts. The past, with its myriad of mistakes, failures, and regrets, no longer defines who you are. You emerge as a new creation with a narrative that is being rewritten. There's something inherently powerful and compelling about the sense of belonging. It's a fundamental human desire – to be a part of something greater than ourselves, to be connected, to be known and yet loved unconditionally. Spiritual adoption fulfills this deep-seated longing. It is God's way of affirming, **"You are now part of My family. You belong with Me."**

This concept is not just a comforting metaphor but a tangible spiritual reality. In Romans 8:15, the Apostle Paul speaks of receiving the "Spirit of adoption." This text implies that the Holy Spirit bears witness to and confirms our new identity as God's children. We are not merely role-playing; we are living out a divine truth.

So, how does one begin to embrace this new identity? The process starts with acceptance – accepting that God has chosen you, complete with all your imperfections and flaws. It's about shedding the old labels that have defined you and stepping into your new role as a child of God. It involves beginning to perceive God not just as a creator or a distant ruler but as a Father – a loving, caring, and deeply invested Father. So, I invite you to open your heart to the profound implications of spiritual adoption. Consider what it means to be chosen, loved, and accepted by the Creator of the universe. Ponder how this new identity can revolutionize how you view yourself, your interactions with others, and your place in the world. Spiritual adoption is a transformative journey that redefines our understanding of identity and belonging. It reshapes our relationship with God, turning it into a more intimate and personal experience. As adopted children, we are not only assured of God's love and care but also entrusted with the responsibility to live out the values and principles of this newfound family. This shift in identity brings a renewed sense of purpose and direction.

The ramifications of spiritual adoption extend beyond our personal lives; they permeate our interactions with others. Recognizing ourselves as God's children encourages us to view others through the same lens of love and acceptance that God has shown us. It fosters a spirit of empathy, kindness, and compassion, urging us to extend the same sense of familial belonging to those around us.

Moreover, spiritual adoption offers a perspective that counters the world's often superficial and transient view of identity. In a world that frequently judges worth based on achievements, appearances, or social status, spiritual adoption grounds our identity in something eternal and unchanging. It reassures us that our value is not contingent upon external factors but is rooted in our inherent worth as children of God. This understanding of spiritual adoption also brings with it a sense of liberation. It frees us from the shackles of past mistakes and the burden of striving for acceptance based on our accomplishments. It provides a safe space of unconditional love and acceptance, allowing us to grow, make mistakes, and evolve without the fear of losing our place in God's family.

By exploring what it means to be spiritually adopted, we are invited to reflect on the profound nature of our relationship with God. This relationship is not transactional; it is relational and built on a foundation of unconditional love and grace. We are called to live in a way that reflects our understanding of this relationship, embodying the values of love, grace, and truth in our daily lives. In this journey of spiritual adoption, we are also encouraged to seek a deeper understanding of God's character. As we grow in our understanding of Him as a Father, our trust in, faith in, and reliance on Him deepens. This journey is about more than understanding a theological concept; it's about experiencing a transformation in how we perceive ourselves, our relationship with God, and our interaction with the world.

Spiritual adoption is a gift of immeasurable value. It offers a fresh start, a new identity, and a secure place in God's eternal family. Moving forward in this journey, let's embrace the fullness of what it means to be God's adopted children. Let's explore together the incredible transformation this brings and how it reshapes our entire understanding of who we are.

THE CHANGE WITHIN

Delving deeper into the exploration of spiritual adoption, a pivotal aspect emerges: transformation. This transformation is not just a superficial change of label; it represents a profound shift that touches the very core of our being. When one experiences spiritual adoption, it is akin to receiving a divine upgrade at the very essence of who they are. This change affects the heart and mind in a profound and deeply personal way. Picture this transformation as a journey where your heart and mind, once clouded by doubts, fears, and confusion, begin to clear. It's akin to seeing the world through a new lens, where everything comes into sharper focus. Suddenly, how you perceive the world, yourself, and even God undergoes a dramatic shift. It's like wearing glasses for the first time – everything that was once blurry now becomes crystal clear. This newfound clarity brings a change in priorities, desires, and perspectives. Your aspirations and longings start to align more with God's will, and your outlook on life receives a heavenly touch.

This transformation, however, isn't always an instant revelation. More often, it's a gradual journey, a process that unfolds over time. It might start with small, almost imperceptible changes in behavior and thought patterns. Perhaps you find yourself exhibiting more patience, showing more love, or finding joy in things that previously went unnoticed. Over time, these changes become more profound, gradually shaping your character, influencing your decisions, and eventually altering your entire way of life. It's important to acknowledge the inner battle that often accompanies this transformation. True change can be challenging; it often requires letting go of familiar habits, comforts, or securities. It might involve confronting difficult truths about oneself or making far-from-easy changes. But in this process of transformation, you're not alone. God's Spirit accompanies you, offering guidance, strength, and encouragement at every step. This divine presence is not just a passive observer but an active participant in your journey of change.

Embracing this new identity that comes with spiritual adoption can be both exhilarating and daunting. You may find yourself grappling with questions like, "Who am I now?" This is a journey of discovery, one where you gradually uncover the person God has always intended you to be. It's about finding your true self, a self that is deeply rooted in Him. This discovery is not a destination but a continuous process that brings new insights and revelations about your identity in God each day. Remember, spiritual transformation is a daily endeavor. It's a conscious choice made each day to live out your identity as God's child. It involves a continual effort to align your will with His and to allow His Spirit to mold and shape you from the inside out. This daily walk is not a path of rigid adherence to rules but a journey of growth, learning, and adaptation.

Reflecting on your life experiences as we explore this transformation is beneficial. Consider where you have witnessed changes since embracing your identity as a child of God. What areas in your life are still undergoing transformation? It's important to approach this self-reflection with patience and an openness to the changes God is bringing about in you. Transformation, especially of a spiritual nature, is rarely a linear process. It involves highs and lows, successes and setbacks. Each step, however, is integral to the journey, contributing to your growth and understanding.

This process of transformation through spiritual adoption is not just about personal growth; it has a ripple effect on your interactions with others. As you undergo this change, your relationships, priorities, and even your contributions to your community can begin to reflect this new identity. You may find yourself more empathetic, compassionate, and inclined to serve and uplift others. This change is not just for your benefit but also for the benefit of those around you, reflecting the love and grace that are at the heart of your spiritual adoption.

Moreover, this transformation fosters a deeper understanding and appreciation of God's nature. As you experience changes within yourself, you gain a more profound insight into the character of God as a loving Father. This understanding enhances your relationship with Him, making it more intimate and meaningful. It helps build a strong foundation of faith that can withstand life's challenges and uncertainties. As you continue this transformative journey, staying connected with a community of believers is crucial. This fellowship can provide support, encouragement, and accountability as you navigate the complexities of spiritual growth. Sharing experiences, learning from others, and engaging in communal worship and prayer can be incredibly enriching and can reinforce the changes you are experiencing.

The journey of transformation through spiritual adoption is one of the most beautiful and challenging aspects of the Christian faith. It is a journey that continually shapes and reshapes our understanding of who we are and who we are meant to be. It challenges us to let go of our old selves and embrace a new identity rooted in God's love and grace. This journey is not just about self-improvement; it's about becoming more like Christ and reflecting His love, compassion, and truth in our everyday lives.

The transformation that comes with spiritual adoption is a holistic and life-changing process. It's a journey that requires patience, perseverance, and a willingness to embrace the new identity that God offers. As we journey through this process, let us do so with open hearts and minds, ready to be transformed and experience the fullness of life God intends for us. Let us embrace this journey not just as individuals but together as a community, supporting and encouraging each other along the way.

THE FATHER-CHILD RELATIONSHIP

Welcome to the heart of our spiritual journey, where we explore our profound and unique relationship with God as our Father. This exploration goes far beyond a mere change in title; it ushers us into a relationship characterized by an unparalleled depth of love, intimacy, and care. Envision the epitome of a loving parent's qualities – warmth, protection, guidance, unconditional love – and then imagine these attributes magnified to an infinite scale. This is a glimpse into our relationship with God as our Father, a bond that transcends our human comprehension of parenthood. It's a connection that is divine, eternal, and deeply personal.

The nature of this divine love is transformative. It has the power to heal, restore, and effect change from the inside out. Regardless of your experiences with earthly fatherhood, whether positive or otherwise, this divine fatherly love is in a league of its own. It fills voids we didn't even realize existed and mends wounds we thought were beyond repair. This father-child relationship with God flourishes through communication, much like any meaningful relationship. In this context, prayer transcends mere petitions; it becomes a profound sharing of your heart and attentive listening to His. It involves being transparent with God, including the chaotic and troubled parts, because He is more than capable of handling it. In these moments of honest, heartfelt communication, you will discover wisdom, comfort, and peace that only He can bestow.

Trust is an integral component of this divine relationship. It entails believing that God has your best interests at heart, even in situations that defy understanding. It's about relying on Him during challenging times and recognizing His constant presence, guiding you through every hurdle. As you nurture this relationship, your perception of God's role in your life becomes more vivid. You begin to discern His guidance, provision, and protection in ways you didn't before. Events that once seemed coincidental now appear as intentional acts of divine orchestration.

I encourage you to delve deeper into this father-child bond with God. Invest time in His presence, seek to understand His heart, and allow His love to shape and transform yours. This relationship is the cornerstone of our spiritual adoption and the wellspring of our true strength, identity, and purpose. This divine father-child relationship transcends the limitations of human love and care. It is a relationship that does not depend on our performance or worthiness; it is rooted in God's unconditional love and grace. In this relationship, we find a safe haven, a place of unconditional acceptance and understanding. God, as our Father, is not only a protector and provider but also a guide and mentor who imparts wisdom and understanding.

In embracing this relationship, we also learn to see ourselves through God's eyes. We begin to understand our worth and value as His children, which can profoundly impact our self-esteem and how we interact with the world. This new perspective helps us navigate life's challenges with a sense of security and confidence, knowing that we are supported and cherished by our heavenly Father. Moreover, this relationship invites us into a deeper level of spiritual maturity. As we grow in our understanding and experience of God's fatherly love, we are also called to emulate these qualities in our interactions with others. This means extending love, forgiveness, and compassion, reflecting the character of our Father in our daily lives.

The journey into understanding and experiencing God's fatherly love is ongoing. It is a path filled with discovery, growth, and transformation. As we continue on this journey, we will encounter moments of profound revelation and deep emotional healing. We will learn to trust God more deeply, to rely on His strength, and to find joy and contentment in His presence. This father-child relationship with God also empowers us to face life's uncertainties and challenges with resilience and hope. It reassures us that we are not alone in our struggles and that we have a Father who is infinitely wise, powerful, and loving. It is a relationship that provides clarity in confusion, strength in weakness, and peace in turmoil. As we engage in this relationship, we also discover the joy of being part of a larger family – the family of God. This realization fosters a sense of belonging and community, connecting us with others who share this same spiritual lineage. It encourages us to support, love, and uplift one another, building each other up in faith and love.

Our spiritual adoption and the father-child relationship with God form the foundation of our faith and identity. This relationship offers us unconditional love, profound healing, and a new way of viewing ourselves and the world. As we embrace this relationship, we are transformed by God's love, finding our true identity, strength, and purpose in Him. So, let us continue to deepen our relationship with our heavenly Father, allowing His love to shape us and guide us on this spiritual journey.

LIVING AS AN ADOPTED CHILD

Now that we've delved into the depths of what it means to be spiritually adopted and the transformative love inherent in our new father-child relationship with God, it's crucial to consider how this affects our daily lives. Understanding our identity as adopted children of God is one thing, but living out this truth is where it truly impacts our existence. This new identity isn't just a spiritual concept; it profoundly changes our everyday actions, decisions, and interactions.

Being an adopted child of God fundamentally alters your worldview. You start to see the world not merely as a place to exist but as a vital part of God's creation, a domain where you play a significant role. This perspective shift leads to seeing people around you not just as strangers or acquaintances but as fellow creations, potential members of this vast divine family. This new way of seeing the world transforms how you interact with it and its inhabitants. Every day, we are faced with numerous choices. As an adopted child of God, these choices assume greater significance. Your decisions are no longer driven solely by personal preference or gain. Instead, they are guided by a desire to honor your Heavenly Father and to reflect His love and goodness in your life. This could manifest in choosing kindness over anger, forgiveness over holding grudges, or integrity over taking the easy way out. It's about aligning your choices with the values and teachings of God, striving to embody them in all aspects of your life.

Living out your identity as God's child is most tangibly expressed through love—love put into action. It's about being present for people, offering help, showing compassion, and reflecting God's love in the world. It involves making your corner of the world brighter, kinder, and more reflective of the heavenly realm. This means actively seeking ways to be a source of positivity and hope in the lives of those you encounter.

This new identity also encompasses growing in your faith. It involves immersing yourself in God's Word, fostering connections with fellow believers, and continuously seeking a deeper understanding of this incredible Father we have. Spiritual growth is an ongoing process with more to learn, experience, and understand.

It's about developing a deeper relationship with God, understanding His nature more fully, and allowing that knowledge to transform you.

This transformed identity has a profound impact on your relationships. It changes how you interact with family, friends, and even colleagues. Your actions and words become influenced by your status as an ambassador for your Heavenly Father. You are no longer living solely for personal gain or satisfaction; you are representing God's love and grace in every interaction and every relationship. As we conclude this chapter on spiritual adoption, it's important to remember that being an adopted child of God isn't just about relishing the benefits; it's about actively living them out. It's about being a beacon of light in the darkness, a vessel of hope and love in a world that is in dire need of both. This identity calls for a proactive approach to life, where your actions, choices, and interactions are consistently reflective of the love and grace you've received.

Looking ahead, our journey takes us into an often misunderstood topic – submission. In the upcoming chapter, "A Son's Submission," we will explore the true meaning of biblical submission, its importance in our walk with God, and how it can be a source of strength and freedom rather than a burden. We'll unpack the nuances of submission, understanding it not as a loss of freedom but as an alignment with God's perfect will and design for our lives. This next step is crucial in understanding the full scope of our relationship with

God and our place in His grand design. Are you ready to continue this journey together? We will embark on a path to deeper understanding and insight. Let's dive into the rich and often challenging concept of submission, exploring how it shapes our relationship with God and impacts our daily walk with Him. This exploration promises to deepen our understanding of our role as God's children and to enhance our spiritual growth. Let's take this next step together with open hearts and minds, ready to learn and grow in our walk with God.

"*NOT MY WILL, BUT YOURS BE DONE.*"

-LUKE 22:42

CHAPTER THREE

A SON'S SUBMISSION

When exploring obedience in our relationship with God, it's important to approach this topic with an open mind. Obedience, especially in the spiritual context, often brings notions of restriction or burden to mind. However, in the grand narrative of our faith, obedience is not about constriction but about finding true liberation and life in its fullest sense.

In our journey as sons of God, the concept of obedience is radically different from the worldly perspective. It isn't about mechanically following a set of rules out of fear or obligation. Instead, it is about aligning our will with God's will, motivated by love and trust. It's about acknowledging and saying, "God, I believe You know what's best for me, and I am ready to follow Your lead." This kind of obedience is deeply rooted in our understanding of God's love for us and His excellent plans for our lives. It's a response that comes from recognizing His wisdom and sovereignty over our lives.

There lies a beautiful paradox at the heart of the Christian faith: In surrender, we find freedom. We encounter unparalleled peace and freedom when we let go of our insistence on controlling every aspect of our lives and place our trust in God's guidance. It's akin to being in the passenger seat with the best driver at the wheel – able to relax and enjoy the journey, secure in the knowledge that you're in capable hands. Obedience, in its purest form, is an act of love. Just as a child trusts and follows their loving parent, our obedience to God is a response to His incredible love for us. It is a way of reciprocating that love, saying, "God, I love You too, and I trust Your heart for me." This obedience is not about fear or compulsion; it's about love and trust, about knowing that the One who calls us to obey is the same One who loves us beyond measure.

When seeking an example of perfect obedience, we need not look further than Jesus Christ. He epitomized a life of complete submission to God's will, even when it led Him to the cross. His obedience wasn't borne out of weakness but emerged from a position of strength, commitment, and love for His Father's plan. It was His love for the Father and humanity that propelled His obedience, making Him the perfect model for us to follow. So, how do we embark on this journey of obedience? The first step is getting to know God – understanding His character, His promises, and His love. The more intimately we know Him, the more we grasp His heart and His desires for us. This knowledge cultivates a natural desire to follow His lead, not because we feel compelled to do so but because our love and trust in Him compels us.

This journey of obedience is also an invitation to trust. While delving deeper into what obedience means and represents, it's worth reflecting on our personal perceptions of obedience. Do we view it as a burden, a set of shackles holding us back? Or do we see it as a pathway to deeper trust, freedom, and fulfillment in God? True obedience is more than a destination; it's a daily walk, a continuous choice to align our lives with God's will and trust Him with our paths. Obedience in the context of our relationship with God involves a dynamic interaction. It's not a one-way street where we blindly follow commands. It's a journey marked by dialogue, understanding, and growth. As we walk this path, we learn more about God's nature, His expectations, and His unending grace. This learning process isn't just intellectual; it's experiential. We learn obedience through the situations we face, the challenges we overcome, and the daily decisions we make.

In understanding obedience, it's crucial to recognize that this journey is not about achieving perfection or adhering to an unattainable standard. It's about progress, about growing each day in our understanding and applying what it means to live obediently. Each step we take, no matter how small, brings us closer to the heart of God and aligns us more closely with His purposes for our lives. Obedience also profoundly impacts our relationships with others. As we learn to obey God, our interactions with those around us are transformed. We begin to see others through God's eyes, treating them with the love, kindness, and grace that flow from an obedient heart. This transformation in our relationships is a testament to the transformative power of living in obedience to God.

Remember that being an adopted child of God isn't just about embracing a new identity; it's about living out that identity in every aspect of our lives. It's about being a light in the darkness, a source of hope and love in a world that desperately needs it. Obedience to God is not a burden; it's a joy and a privilege. It's a journey of discovering the depth of God's love for us and learning to live in a way that honors and reflects that love.

As we delve into the topic of submission, we approach it with an open mind and heart, ready to explore and understand what biblical submission truly means. It's a topic often misunderstood, yet it is crucial in our walk with God. We'll uncover why submission is essential, how it can be a source of strength and freedom, and how it aligns with our identity as God's children. Are you ready to take this next step and delve deeper into the beauty and freedom found in obedience and submission to our Heavenly Father? Let's embark on this journey together, eager to learn, grow, and transform in our walk with God.

SUBMISSION AS STRENGTH

Continuing our journey through the concept of "A Son's Submission," it's crucial to address and challenge a common misconception about submission. Often perceived as a sign of weakness, especially in a world that values autonomy and control, submission within the context of the kingdom of God actually symbolizes strength and wisdom. It's about recognizing the true source of our power and aligning ourselves with it.

The strength in surrender is often underestimated. Consider the immense strength it takes to relinquish your will to someone else's, particularly in a culture that constantly urges us to be in control and prioritize our own desires. Choosing to submit to God's will is a profound declaration of trust and faith. It is an acknowledgment that says, "I believe God's plan is superior to my own." This choice isn't a display of weakness but a manifestation of strength that is rooted in wisdom and deep trust. Throughout the Bible, we see numerous heroes of faith who exhibited remarkable strength through submission. Figures like Abraham, Moses, Esther, and David had pivotal moments when they faced a choice between their own desires and God's will. Their true strength lay not in their capacity to carve their own paths but in their readiness to embrace the path God set for them, even when it was fraught with challenges. In practical, everyday terms, submission can manifest in various forms. It might be as straightforward as beginning your day with prayer, seeking God's guidance in your decisions. Or it could involve making challenging choices that align with God's principles, even when they go against popular opinion. Submission is about continually checking in with God, questioning, "Am I walking in Your will?" It's about making conscious choices that reflect not just our desires but God's desires for us and the world.

Cultivating a heart of submission begins with humility – recognizing that we don't have all the answers and that we require God's direction. It involves immersing ourselves in His Word, understanding His character, and comprehending His heart for us and the world. This process is about building a relationship with God where trust and understanding form the foundation of our decisions and actions. The rewards of living a life of submission are profound. There's an incomparable peace that comes from knowing you are in harmony with God's will. There's a confidence that arises from walking the path He has set and an indescribable joy in witnessing His plans unfold in your life. This peace, confidence, and joy are not fleeting; they are deep-seated and enduring, stemming from a deep connection with the divine.

So, I encourage you to reflect on areas in your life where God might be calling you to a deeper level of surrender. Embracing submission as a form of strength is a journey that demands courage, trust, and an openness to God's leading. It's about redefining what strength looks like – not as self-reliance, but as reliance on God. Are you prepared to redefine submission in your life and experience the strength and wisdom it brings? This journey of embracing submission is not about losing your identity or freedom but finding them in Christ. It's about understanding that in submitting to God, we open ourselves to a life that is richer, deeper, and more aligned with our true purpose.

This journey is not just about following God's will; it's about experiencing a fuller, more meaningful life. It's about discovering the beauty in surrender and the strength in submission. Let's walk this path together, learning, growing, and transforming as we align our will with God's will and embrace the abundant life He offers us through submission.

JESUS - THE ULTIMATE MODEL OF SUBMISSION

To further our understanding of submission in our walk with God, we find the ultimate exemplar in Jesus Christ. His life, an embodiment of perfect submission, offers profound insights into how we can emulate this in our own lives. Jesus' journey was not just about fulfilling a mission; it was a testament to the power and beauty of a life lived in complete submission to God's will.

From the onset of His ministry, Jesus' life was a portrait of submission. This decision was not a passive resignation but an active, deliberate choice made out of deep love and unwavering commitment to God's plan. From teaching in the synagogues to healing the sick and embracing the marginalized, every aspect of His life was in perfect harmony with His Father's will. This alignment was not merely in actions but also in His words, thoughts, and innermost attitudes. Perhaps the most poignant illustration of Jesus' submission is witnessed in the Garden of Gethsemane. Confronted with the imminent agony of crucifixion, He experienced profound distress. Yet, it was in this moment of extreme anguish that He uttered, "*Not my will, but Yours be done*" (Luke 22:42). This statement was far from a mere acceptance of fate; it was a conscious, deliberate embrace of God's grand plan, fully cognizant of the immense cost it entailed.

Jesus' submission was not a product of weakness or an inability to choose otherwise. Instead, it was an act of immense strength and profound love – love for His Father and for humanity. His submission culminated in the greatest act of love known to humanity: the sacrifice on the cross, leading to our salvation. It stands as a powerful testament that true submission can lead to outcomes that change the course of history and the fate of souls. So, what does Jesus' life and example of submission mean for us in practical terms? It beckons us to evaluate our lives and identify areas where we might be resisting full submission to God's will. It challenges us to place our trust in God's plan, even in the face of difficulty or uncertainty, and to derive our strength from aligning ourselves with His divine purposes.

Emulating Jesus' example means that our daily life becomes a journey of continuous submission. This choice involves constantly seeking God's guidance through prayer, aligning our choices with His will, and embodying His teachings and principles in every decision and relationship. It's about making a conscious effort each day to prioritize God's way over our own. Reflecting on Jesus' model of submission invites us to open our hearts to God's voice and direction. A heart and spirit willing to submit to God can lead to extraordinary personal growth, a deepening relationship with Him, and a life that is impactful and driven by purpose. This journey of submission is not always easy. It requires courage to let go of our control, humility to acknowledge our need for God's guidance, and faith to trust in His plan, even when it diverges from our own desires or understanding.

Submission, as exemplified by Jesus, is not about losing our identity or freedom; rather, it is about finding our true identity and freedom in Christ. It's about understanding that our greatest fulfillment and joy come from being in sync with God's will. In Jesus' submission, we find a powerful expression of trust and dependence on the Father, an example that inspires us to entrust our lives to God's wise and loving hands. Our journey of submission also profoundly impacts how we interact with the world around us. Our attitudes and actions towards others are transformed when we align ourselves with God's will. We become more compassionate, patient, and loving, reflecting the character of Christ in our interactions. This transformation not only enriches our lives but also touches the lives of those around us.

In following Jesus' footsteps, we also learn the importance of obedience in the face of trials and suffering. Jesus' path to the cross was not devoid of pain or struggle, yet His submission was unwavering. This teaches us that submission to God does not guarantee a life free from challenges, but it does assure us of God's presence and guidance through every difficulty.

Exploring the concept of submission is an opportunity to reassess our priorities and values. It's a call to examine whether our lives reflect a genuine submission to God's will or if we still hold on to areas where we seek to maintain control. True submission involves a complete surrender, a willingness to lay our plans, hopes, and even fears at God's feet, trusting in His perfect plan for our lives. This journey of understanding and practicing submission is transformative. It molds us into the individuals God intends us to be, helps us grow in our faith, and enables us to experience the fullness of life in Christ. It's a journey that requires a daily commitment to walk in obedience and faith, relying not on our own understanding but on God's infinite wisdom and love.

As we move forward in this chapter and in our lives, let us embrace the journey of submission with a spirit of trust and openness. Let us look to Jesus, our ultimate example of submission, and find in His life the inspiration and guidance we need to live lives fully submitted to God. In doing so, we step into a life of true freedom, purpose, and joy, a life that is rich in meaning and abundant in the blessings that come from walking in close fellowship with our Heavenly Father.

SUBMISSION DAILY

Understanding how we can translate the grand biblical narratives of submission into the practical, everyday aspects of our lives is crucial. Submission isn't just a concept reserved for the great heroes of faith or significant life events; it can be woven into the fabric of our daily existence.

Each day offers a new canvas for practicing submission. A great place to start is with prayer. Rather than treating it as just another item on your daily checklist, approach prayer as a genuine conversation with God. Mornings can be transformed into moments of alignment, where you seek God's guidance for the day ahead. This conversation isn't just about asking for things but seeking the wisdom and strength to follow His lead, even in the small, seemingly mundane aspects of life.

Another practical tool for cultivating a spirit of submission is regular engagement with the Bible. The Scriptures serve as a compass, offering wisdom, guidance, and inspiration for living a life submitted to God. Let the Bible shape your thoughts, actions, and decisions. It's about letting God's Word inform and transform your daily life, aligning your path with His teachings and principles.

Submission also plays a crucial role in decision-making. With every choice, big or small, take a moment to consider God's perspective. Ask yourself, "Does this choice reflect God's will and His teachings?" Sometimes, this might lead you down a path less traveled or to decisions that might not align with popular opinion but resonate with the principles and values that God upholds.

Regarding relationships – be it with family, friends, or colleagues – submission means approaching each interaction with the love, humility, and selflessness that Jesus modeled. It means listening more, extending grace, and considering others' needs, sometimes even above your own. It's about embodying the love of Christ in how we treat and interact with those around us.

Challenges and difficulties, too, are integral parts of this journey of submission. Instead of viewing them as obstacles, see them as opportunities to deepen your trust and reliance on God. When pushed out of your comfort zone, lean not on your own understanding but on the strength and guidance that comes from God.

At the end of each day, a reflective practice can be incredibly valuable. Take some time to consider moments where you were able to submit to God's will successfully and areas where you found it challenging. Use these reflections as a means to grow, to recommit to walking in obedience, and to learn from your experiences.

Remember, submission is not a one-time event but a continuous journey. It's about progressively growing in your relationship with God, learning to trust Him more deeply each day, and allowing His will to shape and mold you into the person He desires you to be. This journey is one of transformation, where we gradually align more closely with God's will and purpose for our lives.

As we close this chapter and look forward to the next, we transition from the theme of submission to the practice of service. In the upcoming chapter, 'The Service of a Son,' we will explore how our submission to God's will naturally leads us into service. This service is not just about fulfilling duties; it's an expression of our sonship, an extension of our relationship with God. We will delve into how serving God and others can be fulfilling and integral to living out our faith.

In the context of submission, service is about putting our faith into action. It's about living out the principles and values we've embraced, not just in words but in deeds. As we prepare to explore this aspect of our faith, get ready to discover the profound joy and fulfillment that comes from serving – serving not out of obligation but out of love and submission to God. It's a journey that promises to enrich your faith and deepen your understanding of what it means to live as a child of God, fully submitted and dedicated to His purpose.

SERVICE IS AN ACT OF WORSHIP.

CHAPTER FOUR

THE $\mathscr{S}$ERVICE OF A SON

I n this chapter, our focus shifts from the discipline of submission to the act of service. In God's kingdom, being a son is intrinsically linked to service. This concept of service is not merely about abstaining from certain actions in submission; it's about what we actively choose to do in service.

One of the most exhilarating aspects of our spiritual journey is the discovery of our unique role in God's plan. Each of us is endowed with specific talents, gifts, and passions, carefully woven into our being by God for a purpose. Your calling is the intersection where your abilities and the world's needs meet. It's like having a personal mission field, designated and blessed by God, where you can make a significant impact.

Service, in the Christian context, is far more than a mere obligation or a task to be checked off a list. It is a profound reflection of our identity as God's children. We emulate Jesus, who came not to be served but to serve others. Our service becomes a concrete demonstration of God's love for those around us, an act that extends the grace and compassion we have received from Him. Contrary to the notion that service is draining or demanding, true service is a source of joy and fulfillment when aligned with our calling. It's not about reluctantly parting with our time or resources. Instead, it's about enthusiastically investing in the work God has prepared for us, finding happiness and satisfaction in being part of His grand design.

The journey of service begins with seeking God's guidance. Start with prayer, earnestly asking God to reveal where He desires you to serve. This calling might be within your local church, community, or even your workplace. Stay open to His leading, even if it directs you beyond your comfort zone.

Take some time to introspect and discover your unique gifts and talents. Reflect on what you excel at and what brings you joy, and consider how these abilities can be utilized to bless others and glorify God. Sometimes, the calling God has for you is hidden in the things you naturally excel at and enjoy, waiting to be recognized and put into action.

Once you have an inkling of where God is calling you, step out in faith. It doesn't require a grandiose action to start; small steps are just as significant. The magnitude of service is not what counts most; it's the intention and the heart behind it. Even the smallest act of service, done in love and faith, can have a profound impact. Moving forward, consider service not as a duty but as an adventure. This adventure is an opportunity to witness God working through you in remarkable ways. It's a chance to not just do good but to live out the divine purpose for which you were created. Embracing service as a son of God is about embarking on an enriching journey, where you discover the joy, satisfaction, and purpose that comes from serving others in God's name.

This journey of service is as varied and unique as each individual. It could manifest in various forms – from volunteering at a local shelter, mentoring young people, participating in community projects, to simple acts of kindness in everyday interactions. Every act of service, no matter how small, contributes to the larger tapestry of God's kingdom work.

Service also involves being attentive to the needs around us. It's about having the sensitivity to notice when someone is struggling and the willingness to offer help. It's being the hands and feet of Jesus in a world that desperately needs compassion and love. This service isn't just beneficial to those we help; it enriches our own lives, drawing us closer to God and giving us a deeper understanding of His heart for humanity.

Moreover, service is an act of worship. It's a way to express our gratitude to God for all He has done for us by extending His love to others. It's an acknowledgment that everything we have – our talents, resources, and time – are gifts from God, meant to be used for His glory and the betterment of His creation.

As we continue this journey, let's embrace the challenges and opportunities that come with service. Let's be open to learning, growing, and being transformed as we serve. Each experience of service is an opportunity to reflect on God's character, grow in our faith, and deepen our understanding of what it means to live as obedient children of God.

THE JOY OF SERVICE

Welcome to the heart of service, where the concept of duty transforms into an experience of delight. In our journey of faith, service is often viewed as a responsibility, something we ought to do as part of our commitment to God and others. However, there is a deeper, more enriching layer to service – one where it becomes a source of profound joy and fulfillment. This layer is where the act of serving transcends mere obligation and becomes a conduit for receiving unexpected blessings.

There's a certain magic that happens when you engage in service. It's not about depleting your resources or losing a part of yourself; rather, it's about discovering aspects of your character and capabilities that you might not have known existed. This discovery could manifest in various forms, such as volunteering at a local food bank, mentoring a young person, or simply being there for a friend in need. Each of these acts of service can imbue you with a sense of purpose and joy that is difficult to find in other pursuits.

No matter how seemingly small, every act of service creates ripples that extend far beyond the immediate action. The full impact of your service may not always be visible to you, but rest assured, your actions can inspire hope, provoke positive change, and spread kindness in ways that go far beyond your immediate environment. It's like planting and watching seeds of goodness flourish in ways you might never have anticipated.

Service doesn't always have to appear grand or heroic. More often than not, service is found in the ordinary, everyday acts of kindness and consideration. It's in the smile you share with a stranger, the patience you exhibit in a stressful situation, or the time you dedicate to listening to someone who needs to be heard. These seemingly small acts of service can bring unexpected joy to both the giver and the receiver.

However, it's crucial to maintain a balance in serving others. It's important to serve from a place of strength and not from a point of depletion. This means taking care of your own needs as well, ensuring that you are at your best when serving others. After all, you can't pour from an empty cup. Ensuring your own well-being is not selfish; it's necessary to be an effective and compassionate servant.

Each opportunity to serve is also an opportunity to learn about others, the world, and yourself. These experiences are invaluable, offering insights and growth that can only be gained through the act of giving and connecting with others. Embracing service with an open heart and mind allows you to discover new perspectives, understand different life situations, and grow in empathy and understanding.

As we delve further into this chapter, I invite you to rethink the concept of service. Consider it not as a chore or an obligation but as a pathway to joy and personal fulfillment. Look for opportunities to serve in your daily routine and approach them with enthusiasm and openness. Be ready to experience the unique joy that comes from positively impacting someone else's life.

Service, in its truest form, celebrates our interconnectedness and our ability to positively impact each other's lives. It's about recognizing that in helping others, we also help ourselves in profound and often unexpected ways. The joy of service lies in the understanding that our actions, no matter how small, can make a significant difference.

This joy of service extends beyond individual acts. It permeates our communities, creating a culture of care, kindness, and support. When we engage in service, we contribute to building a community that values and practices compassion and altruism. This act not only enhances the lives of individuals within the community but also strengthens the community as a whole.

Moreover, service is a reflection of our gratitude. It's a way of expressing thanks for the blessings and grace we have received. By serving others, we acknowledge the gifts we have been given and commit to sharing them with those around us. This act of giving back is both a recognition of what we have received and a commitment to pay it forward.

In addition to being a source of joy and personal growth, service is a testament to our faith. It's a practical demonstration of the values and teachings we hold dear. In serving others, we live out the teachings of Christ, showing love, kindness, and compassion in action. This alignment of our actions with our beliefs is a powerful form of witness, showcasing the transformative power of faith in our lives and the lives of others.

As we progress through this chapter and reflect on our personal experiences with service, let's challenge ourselves to find joy in every act of service, no matter how small. Let's approach each opportunity to serve with a spirit of enthusiasm, ready to experience the fulfillment and happiness that come from selflessly giving to others.

Service is not just a duty; it's a privilege and an opportunity for joy and personal growth. It's a journey that enriches our lives, deepens our faith, and connects us with others in meaningful and lasting ways. So, let's embrace this journey of service with open hearts and minds, ready to discover the abundant joy and fulfillment that come from living out our faith through acts of kindness, compassion, and service.

JESUS - CHIEF SERVANT

Delving deeper into understanding service in the context of our Christian walk, our attention naturally turns to Jesus Christ – the ultimate example of what it means to be a servant. His life was not solely about preaching powerful messages or performing awe-inspiring miracles; at its core, it was about serving others. In Jesus, we find the quintessential model of a servant leader, an exemplar whose life encapsulates the essence of true service.

Jesus' approach to service was nothing short of revolutionary. He demonstrated this most poignantly when He washed His disciples' feet, a task traditionally reserved for servants. This act was not just a display of humility but a powerful lesson in the importance of serving others, irrespective of their status or position in society. Furthermore, His interactions with those marginalized by society underscored that service knows no boundaries and is not confined by societal norms or expectations. Jesus embodied selfless love and compassion in every action and interaction, setting a precedent for what service should look like.

One of the most striking attributes of Jesus' service was His deep-seated compassion. He didn't just see the physical needs of the people around Him; He also perceived their spiritual and emotional needs. He listened attentively, healed the sick, comforted the distressed, and uplifted the downtrodden. His service was a holistic response to humanity's multifaceted needs.

Following in Jesus' footsteps means being willing to step out of our comfort zones to serve others. It's about serving not only those who are easy to love but also those who may challenge us. It's about looking beyond the surface, seeing people through the compassionate eyes of Jesus, and reaching out with a heart full of His love and grace.

Jesus' life and actions present a call to active service. It's insufficient to simply admire His teachings or be moved by His examples of compassion; we are called to embody and live out these principles. This means actively seeking opportunities to serve – in our families, communities, and wider contexts. According to Jesus' example, service is not just an activity; it's a way of life, a fundamental aspect of our Christian identity.

The impact of Christlike service extends beyond meeting immediate needs. When we serve as Jesus did, we do more than just address physical or emotional needs; we become conduits of God's love and grace. This kind of service has a transformative power—it changes the lives of those we serve and also changes us. It draws us closer to God, aligning our hearts with His and molding us into the people He desires us to be.

Embracing the servant heart of Jesus is key as we go forth on our journey. We are encouraged to reflect on how we can incorporate His approach to service into our daily lives. Consider how you can demonstrate compassion, step outside your comfort zone, and actively serve those around you. Think about how you can be a blessing in both big and small ways and how each act of service can reflect the love and compassion of Christ.

Service, as demonstrated by Jesus, is not limited to grand gestures. It often manifests in simple, everyday actions. Service is found in the patience we show, the kindness we offer, and the understanding we extend. It's in the moments we choose to listen rather than speak, to offer help without being asked, and to give without expecting anything in return.

Furthermore, Jesus' example teaches us that service is not about self-promotion or seeking recognition. It's about humility, about serving quietly and faithfully, often without fanfare or acknowledgment. It's about doing what is right and loving, not what is convenient or self-serving.

As we strive to follow Jesus' example, we are reminded that service is also about building relationships – with those we serve, with fellow believers, and with God Himself. It's about creating connections that reflect God's love and grace, building community, and being the hands and feet of Jesus in a world in need.

In our service, we are also called to be mindful and discerning. It's about understanding the needs of those we serve and responding in ways that are truly helpful and empowering. It's about listening to the guidance of the Holy Spirit and being responsive to His leading in our service endeavors.

Remember that to serve as Jesus did is to participate in the work of the Kingdom of God. It's about bringing light into darkness, hope into despair, and love into places where it is desperately needed. Let's embrace the joy and challenge of service, carrying the servant heart of Jesus into every aspect of our lives and making service a natural and joyful expression of our faith. Let's step into the adventure of service, ready to experience the fulfillment and joy that come from following the ultimate example set by Jesus, our Savior and Lord.

SERVICE IN ACTION

Entering the chapter's concluding section, our focus shifts from the theoretical understanding of service to its practical application in our everyday lives. Service, in its essence, is not just a concept to be understood but a practice to be lived out. It's about translating the principles of service into tangible actions that impact both our lives and the lives of those around us.

The first step in turning theory into practice is identifying opportunities for service in your daily life. These opportunities can be as simple as helping a neighbor with groceries, volunteering in community projects, or offering a listening ear to a friend in distress. Service doesn't have to be a grand gesture to be meaningful; often, it's the small acts of kindness that leave the most significant impact.

Look at your immediate sphere - family, friends, workplace, and community - for opportunities to serve. How can you be of service in these areas? It might involve being more patient and understanding with family members, offering support and encouragement to a colleague at work, or participating in local community initiatives. Each environment presents unique opportunities to contribute positively and make a difference. Another key aspect of service is utilizing your God-given gifts and talents. Each of us is equipped with unique abilities and skills that can be used to serve others. If you're skilled at teaching, consider tutoring students who need extra help. If you have a passion for cooking, perhaps you can prepare meals for those in need. Your talents and abilities are not just for personal achievement; they are gifts meant to be shared and used to serve others.

It's important to remember that the impact of your service can extend far beyond the immediate act. What may seem like a small gesture to you can significantly affect someone else's life. Moreover, acts of service often create a ripple effect, inspiring and encouraging others to engage in acts of kindness and service in their own ways.

While being committed to service, it's also vital to balance it with self-care. Serving others effectively requires serving from a place of personal well-being. It's not selfish to take care of yourself; rather, it's essential. Ensuring that you are physically, mentally, and spiritually healthy allows you to continue positively impacting others.

Ultimately, service is more than just an activity—it's a lifestyle. It involves adopting a mindset that consistently seeks ways to positively contribute to others' lives. It's about integrating service into the fabric of your daily existence, making it a natural and integral part of your identity as a child of God.

As we wrap up this chapter on service and prepare for the next, we stand at the threshold of deepening our understanding of what it means to be a son in God's kingdom. The upcoming chapter, "Heir - A Son's Birthright," will delve into the concept of spiritual inheritance and what it means to be an heir in God's kingdom. We will explore the fullness of what we've been given as children of God, examining the privileges, responsibilities, and the profound identity that comes with our sonship.

Understanding our birthright as God's children promises to be enlightening, inspiring, and transformative. It will take us deeper into the heart of what it means to be part of God's family and the inheritance that awaits us in His kingdom. So, are you ready to take this next step? Let's embark on this journey together, eager to discover the depths of our identity and inheritance as sons of God.

BEING AN *HEIR*
IS NOT
A PASSIVE IDENTITY.

CHAPTER FIVE

HEIR: A SON'S BIRTHRIGHT

Chapter 5 explores one of the most profound aspects of being a child of God: our spiritual inheritance. This journey isn't about acquiring physical wealth or material possessions; it's about exploring something far more valuable and enduring. This spiritual inheritance transcends the conventional concept of wealth, offering us eternal and immeasurable treasures.

In the Bible, the concept of inheritance often pertained to tangible assets like land, wealth, or possessions passed from one generation to the next. However, when we speak of our inheritance as God's children, we enter a different realm altogether. We're talking about eternal life, boundless love, unfailing grace, and the ever-present indwelling of the Holy Spirit. These gifts are the true inheritance that awaits us – gifts that transcend monetary value and are impervious to the decay of time and death.

This spiritual inheritance is incomparable to any earthly riches we might chase. It encompasses having access to God's wisdom in our daily decisions, His strength in our moments of weakness, and His peace amidst life's tumult. It's about the assurance that, regardless of life's uncertainties, we have a Heavenly Father who is committed to providing for, protecting, and empowering us.

What makes this inheritance even more extraordinary is how it was secured – through the life, death, and resurrection of Jesus Christ. His ultimate sacrifice opened the way for us to be part of God's family and to partake in this magnificent inheritance. It's a testament to a love so profound that it is freely given, not earned.

Embracing our identity as heirs of God means viewing ourselves and our lives through the lens of this spiritual wealth. It involves living with the confidence and assurance that stem from knowing we are valued, cared for, and provided for by God. It's about walking in the authority and freedom that come from understanding our worth and place in the Father's heart.

As heirs, we are also called to stewardship of this inheritance. This responsibility entails utilizing the gifts and resources God has bestowed upon us to serve others and further His kingdom. It's not merely about enjoying the privileges of our inheritance; it's about sharing it. We are called to spread the love, grace, and hope we have received to those around us.

I invite you to open your heart to the fullness of what it means to be an heir in God's kingdom as we delve deeper into exploring the depths of our spiritual inheritance in this chapter. This journey is one of discovery, replete with awe and wonder at the lavish generosity of our Heavenly Father. It's about uncovering the immense treasures that form our spiritual birthright.

This exploration is not just an intellectual exercise; it's a transformative experience. Understanding our spiritual inheritance can change how we perceive ourselves, our relationships, and our purpose in life. It can shift our priorities, influence our decisions, and inspire us to live in a way that honors this inheritance.

Our spiritual inheritance also shapes our understanding of God's nature. It reveals His character as a loving, generous, and faithful Father who delights in blessing His children. It helps us trust Him more deeply, rely on His promises, and rest in the security of His provision and care.

Furthermore, this journey into understanding our inheritance is about recognizing the communal aspect of this gift. We are not isolated heirs; we are part of a family – the family of God. This realization calls us to live in fellowship with our brothers and sisters in Christ, to support, encourage, and uplift one another as we all partake in this shared inheritance.

As we continue in this chapter, let's approach this exploration with a sense of anticipation and eagerness. Let's be ready to uncover the rich treasures of our spiritual inheritance and embrace the fullness of what it means to be an heir in God's kingdom. This journey is not just about understanding our rights and privileges as God's children but also about living in a manner that reflects our gratitude and reverence for this incredible gift.

As heirs of God, we have been given a legacy that is eternal, unfading, and full of glory. It's a legacy that shapes our identity, directs our life's path, and empowers us to live in the fullness of God's plan for us. So, let's embark on this journey together, ready to dive deep into the treasures of our birthright and discover the richness of being sons of the Most High. Let's go!

A NEW PERSPECTIVE

While exploring the birthright of believers, we encounter a significant shift in understanding from the traditional notion of a birthright in biblical times. Historically, a birthright was a special honor reserved for the firstborn son, symbolizing both authority and a double portion of the inheritance. However, within the context of our faith, this concept of birthright is transformed into something new and far more inclusive.

In Christ, the conventional idea of the birthright is redefined. It's no longer about birth order or family lineage; instead, it's about our position as children of God. Every believer, irrespective of their background or the time of their coming to faith, is entitled to this spiritual birthright. This idea marks a radical shift from a framework of exclusion to one of inclusion, expanding the scope from what was once limited to something boundless.

What, then, does this birthright entail for us as believers? It encompasses our status as co-heirs with Christ (Romans 8:17), meaning that we share in His inheritance. This inheritance isn't limited to the promise of eternal life, the presence of the Holy Spirit, and access to the kingdom of God; it also includes our identity, authority, and mission as integral members of God's family.

Our birthright is more than a future hope; it's a present reality with practical implications for our daily lives. It shapes how we live today, how we engage with the world, and how we continue the legacy of faith. As bearers of this birthright, we are called to live as ambassadors of God's kingdom, exemplifying what it means to be a part of His family to the world.

With this birthright, however, comes significant responsibility. It is not merely a privilege but a call to action. We are charged with stewarding the gifts and promises bestowed upon us, utilizing them to glorify God and serve others. This stewardship involves deepening our faith, sharing the gospel, and embodying God's love and grace in tangible, impactful ways.

Embracing our birthright as believers means acknowledging and accepting both the privileges and responsibilities it entails. It's about seeing ourselves as God sees us: valued, empowered, and entrusted with a purpose. It's about stepping into our roles with confidence and faith, trusting that God will guide us and use us for His glory.

While reflecting on the concept of the birthright of believers, it's important to consider what this means for our own lives. How does understanding your birthright alter your perspective on your identity, your purpose, and your everyday actions? This birthright is not just a theological concept; it's a transformative reality that should shape our worldview, self-perception, and interactions with others.

Understanding our birthright also changes how we view our relationship with God. It's about recognizing that we are not distant, disconnected beings but intimately connected to our Heavenly Father, deeply loved and valued by Him. This understanding brings a sense of belonging, security, and assurance that we are part of something greater than ourselves – a divine family with a rich heritage and a glorious future.

Moreover, this birthright influences our sense of community with other believers. As co-heirs with Christ, we share a common identity and destiny. This shared birthright calls us to unity, mutual support, and a collective pursuit of God's purposes. It invites us to engage with our church and faith communities not just as members but as active, contributing participants in God's kingdom work.

Furthermore, embracing our birthright means recognizing our role in the broader narrative of God's redemptive plan. We are not passive recipients of God's blessings but active participants in His mission. This involvement calls for a commitment to live out the values of the Kingdom, to be agents of change and reconciliation in a broken world, and to bear witness to the gospel's transformative power.

As we continue this journey of discovery, let's embrace the fullness of our birthright in Christ. Let's explore what it means to live as heirs of God's kingdom, to fully engage with the privileges and responsibilities this entails, and to step into the roles God has prepared for us. This journey is one of empowerment, purpose, and transformation, inviting us to live out our faith in dynamic and impactful ways.

Our birthright as believers is a profound aspect of our identity in Christ. It's a call to live with an awareness of our spiritual wealth, to steward the gifts and opportunities God has given us, and to engage with the world from a place of strength, purpose, and love. As we move forward, let's do so with a renewed understanding of our birthright, ready to live as true heirs of God's kingdom, embracing and fulfilling the extraordinary calling He has placed on our lives.

LIVING AS HEIRS

In understanding our role as heirs in God's kingdom, it is crucial to maintain a balanced perspective on the privileges and responsibilities that accompany our spiritual birthright. This inheritance is more than just a passive receipt of blessings; it actively shapes how we live and conduct ourselves as God's children.

Firstly, let's consider the privileges of being heirs. We have the privilege of direct access to God's presence, His guidance, and His comfort. We are assured of His unending love and protection and have the promise of eternal life. These are not merely distant hopes but present realities that profoundly influence our lives, providing us with a sense of security and belonging within God's family.

However, these incredible privileges are accompanied by significant responsibilities. As heirs, we are called to live in a manner that honors our Heavenly Father. This act entails pursuing a life characterized by righteousness, integrity, and love. It means representing God's kingdom honorably, serving as His ambassadors on Earth, and spreading His message of hope and salvation to others.

An integral part of our responsibility as heirs involves stewarding what we have been given. This stewardship extends to our time, talents, and resources. It prompts us to reflect on how we utilize these gifts to serve others and contribute to the growth of God's kingdom. Effective stewardship is an expression of our gratitude and a recognition of the value of our inheritance.

Being an heir also necessitates actively living out our faith. It's not a passive identity but a dynamic and engaging lifestyle. It's about making choices that reflect our faith, serving others selflessly, and consistently growing in our relationship with God. This active living is a testament to our commitment to God and our understanding of our role as heirs.

The way we live as heirs has a powerful impact. We have the opportunity to influence those around us, shine as lights in the darkness, and exemplify God's love and grace. How we manage our inheritance can draw others to Christ and effect lasting change in the world.

As we reflect on the dual aspects of being heirs—the privileges and the responsibilities—let's consider how this understanding influences our daily lives. Are we living in a way that honors the inheritance we have received? Are we effectively stewarding the gifts and calling bestowed upon us?

In embracing the fullness of our role as heirs, we should live with purpose, gratitude, and a heart for service. This means enjoying the benefits of our spiritual inheritance and using them to make a positive difference in the world. It's about recognizing that our inheritance is not just for our own benefit but is meant to be shared and used to bless others.

Furthermore, as heirs, we have a unique opportunity to showcase a different way of living—one that is counter to the selfishness and self-centeredness that often characterize the world. By living as true heirs, we demonstrate the virtues of generosity, kindness, and selflessness. We show that our lives are not driven by a pursuit of personal gain but by a desire to reflect the character of our Heavenly Father.

Our inheritance also calls us to be agents of reconciliation and peace. As heirs, we carry the message of reconciliation between God and humanity, extending this reconciliation to our relationships and interactions with others. We are called to be peacemakers, to foster unity, and to build bridges in a divided world.

Moving forward, let's commit to living out this identity in every aspect of our lives as we explore and understand our inheritance as believers. Let's embrace both the joys and the challenges that come with being heirs, using our inheritance to glorify God, serve others, and better the world. Let's take up the mantle of our spiritual birthright with dedication and joy, ready to live as true heirs of God's kingdom, fulfilling the purposes He has for us with faithfulness and love.

CLAIMING YOUR INHERITANCE

Understanding how we can actively claim and embrace our spiritual inheritance as children of God is pivotal. It is not about passive acceptance; it involves actively stepping into the roles and privileges God has laid out for us.

The first step in claiming your inheritance is acknowledging your status in Christ. It is crucial to recognize that you are not merely a believer but a child of God and an heir to His kingdom. This acknowledgment goes beyond mere intellectual assent; it's about a heart acceptance that fundamentally changes how you perceive yourself and your place in the world. It's about seeing yourself through the lens of God's love and promise, understanding the depth of your relationship with Him and the privileges that come with it.

Understanding the depth of your inheritance is another vital step. Delve into the Scriptures to comprehend the full scope of what you have inherited. This inheritance includes promises of God's continual presence, His guidance in your life, the peace that surpasses all understanding, and the assurance of eternal life. The more deeply you understand your inheritance, the more it becomes a reality in your everyday life.

Begin to live in the reality of this inheritance. It means walking in faith, holding onto God's promises even amidst challenging circumstances, and letting the truth of your identity as God's heir influence your decisions, actions, and outlook on life. It's about embodying the confidence and assurance that comes from knowing you are a beloved child of God.

Sharing your inheritance with others is also a key part of claiming it. Your inheritance is not just for your own enjoyment; your inheritance is meant to be shared. Use your gifts, talents, and resources to bless others. Demonstrate the love, grace, and mercy you have received with those around you, reflecting the generosity of God in your actions and interactions.

Claiming your inheritance also involves continual growth and maturity in your spiritual life. It's a lifelong journey of becoming more like Christ, learning to trust God more profoundly, and allowing the Holy Spirit to work within and through you. This growth process involves learning from the Word of God and applying its truths to your life.

Embrace your role in God's kingdom as part of claiming your inheritance. As an heir, you have a significant part to play in God's redemptive plan for the world. This role could involve serving in various capacities in your local church, engaging in missions, or being a godly influence within your community and spheres of influence.

As we wrap up this chapter on our birthright as heirs, let's look ahead to the next exciting aspect of our identity in Christ. The upcoming chapter, "The Commission of a Son," will delve into the concept of divine commissioning and what it means for our lives. This exploration is about understanding and stepping into the specific purpose God has for each of us. It's an invitation to discover how God wants to use us uniquely in His grand narrative.

Are you prepared to explore more about your divine commission? This next chapter promises to be a journey of discovery, where we delve into understanding the unique calling and purpose God has placed on each of our lives. It's about moving from knowing who we are in Christ to living out that identity in the world. Let's embark on this journey together, eager to uncover and embrace God's commission for each of us as His beloved children.

CHAPTER SIX

A SON'S COMMISSION

In this chapter, we embark on the exciting exploration of divine commissioning. This journey is not merely about discovering your purpose; it's about understanding and embracing the specific mission God has entrusted to you as His heir. This section is about unraveling what divine commissioning entails and how you can identify and embrace your unique calling in God's kingdom.

Divine commissioning is essentially God's personal invitation for you to undertake a specific role or task within His kingdom. It's akin to receiving a special assignment directly from the CEO of the universe, tailored uniquely to you. This calling is distinctive and molded to fit your talents, experiences, and spiritual gifts.

So, how do you identify your divine commission? The process begins with prayer and maintaining a heart that is open and responsive to God's guidance. Seek clarity from God on the role He has envisioned for you. Often, this commission is linked to your passions and burdens – the issues or needs that deeply move and concern you.

Understanding your spiritual gifts is a key component in discerning your divine commission. These gifts are the tools God has equipped you with to fulfill your calling. They could range from teaching, encouragement, and leadership to service, among others. Recognizing and understanding these gifts can provide significant insights into the nature of your calling.

The life of Jesus Christ offers the perfect example of understanding and living out a divine commission. Jesus was acutely aware that His mission was to seek and save the lost (Luke 19:10). His entire life and ministry on earth were intricately aligned with this purpose. In the same way, we are called to discern, understand, and live out our divine commission.

Discovering your divine commission is a deeply personal and spiritual journey. It involves intimate communion with God, immersing yourself in His Word, and being sensitive to the nudges of the Holy Spirit. It's about being alert to the opportunities God places in your path and the doors He opens in your life.

Embracing your divine commission means stepping out in faith, sometimes even when the path ahead isn't fully clear. It's about trusting in God's omniscience – His knowledge of your abilities and His provision for your task. This journey is an adventure marked by faith, obedience, and the pursuit of fulfillment.

So, I encourage you to reflect on what God might be calling you to do as we examine the concept of divine commission. Consider how your unique blend of gifts, experiences, and passions can be utilized to serve God and impact the lives of others. Are you prepared to uncover and embrace your divine commission? Let's embark on this journey with open hearts and minds, ready to discover and fulfill God's specific purpose for each of us in His grand plan.

This exploration of divine commissioning is not just about personal fulfillment; it's about contributing to something greater than ourselves. It's about understanding that each of us has a role to play in God's kingdom, an integral and significant part. As we seek to discover our commission, we align ourselves with God's overarching mission and become active participants in His redemptive work.

Moreover, embracing your divine commission requires a willingness to grow and adapt. As you step into your calling, you may encounter challenges and opportunities that require you to develop new skills, deepen your knowledge, or even step into unfamiliar territories. It's a process that calls for humility, a willingness to learn, and an openness to God's shaping and refining.

As heirs and children of God, our commission is also intertwined with our identity in Christ. It's about living out the values and teachings of Jesus, embodying His character, and reflecting His love and grace in all that we do. Our commission is not separate from our identity; it's an expression of who we are in Christ and a manifestation of our relationship with Him.

Throughout this chapter, let's explore the concept of divine commissioning with anticipation and eagerness. Let's be ready to embrace the unique calling God has for each of us, to step into our roles with faith and courage, and to live out our commission with passion and dedication. This journey is not just about finding our purpose; it's about living it out in a way that glorifies God, serves others, and fulfills the calling He has placed upon our lives.

NAVIGATING GOD'S PLAN

Now that we've started to grasp the concept of divine commissioning, it's time to explore how to fulfill this unique calling. Navigating God's plan for your life is an adventure that demands faith, perseverance, and a readiness to follow His guidance, even when it leads into uncharted territories. Here are six principles that you can use as a guide to navigate the journey of fulfilling your purpose.

1. Embrace Faith Over Fear Stepping into your divine commission often requires moving beyond your comfort zone. Facing fear and doubt is a natural part of this journey, but faith becomes crucial here. Trusting in God's promise that He will equip and guide you is essential. As stated in 2 Timothy 1:7, "*For God has not* *given us a spirit of fear, but of power and of love and of a sound mind.* " Embrace this assurance and let faith overshadow your fears.

2. Seek Wisdom and Guidance Continuously seek God's wisdom and guidance as you pursue your commission. This pursuit can be through dedicated prayer, consulting with trusted spiritual mentors, and immersing yourself in the Word of God. Be open to receiving His direction in various forms and be prepared for it to sometimes come in unexpected ways.

3. Take Practical Steps Faith and trust in God's guidance should be complemented with practical actions. This might mean further education, acquiring new skills, building relevant relationships, or making significant changes in your career or personal life. Each step, taken under God's guidance, brings you closer to fulfilling your calling.

4. Persevere Through Challenges The path of divine commission is not always smooth; it is often laden with challenges and setbacks. It's important to persevere through these times, recognizing them as part of God's refining process. James 1:12 encourages us with, *"Blessed is the one who perseveres under trial. "*

5. Celebrate Small Victories Acknowledge and give thanks for every small step of progress. Celebrating these victories, regardless of their size, is important as they are markers of God's faithfulness and your dedication to

His call.

6. Remain Flexible and Open Be adaptable and open to changes along your journey. God's plan may unfold differently than your expectations. Being willing to modify your plans or expectations in response to God's guidance is key to faithfully following your divine commission.

Fulfilling your divine commission is a continuous journey with God. It involves partnering with Him in His work, growing in your faith, and making an impact in the world in your own unique way. As you navigate this path, keep your heart and ears attuned to God's leading. Be ready for the incredible ways He will use you to further His kingdom.

This journey of divine commissioning is about more than just personal fulfillment; it's about participating in God's larger story. It's a call to live out the gospel in practical, tangible ways, impacting lives and communities. As you step into your commission, remember that you are part of a grand narrative that God is weaving through history.

Venturing further through this chapter and beyond, let's approach our divine commission with a heart full of faith, a spirit ready for adventure, and a willingness to be used by God in extraordinary ways. Let's embrace the challenges and joys of this journey, knowing that we are fulfilling God's purpose for our lives and contributing to His redemptive plan for the world. Let's step forward in faith, ready for the remarkable journey God has in store for each of us as His commissioned children.

BIBLICAL EXAMPLES OF COMMISSION

In this crucial section, we turn to the lives of biblical figures to draw inspiration and learn valuable lessons about fulfilling our divine commission. The experiences of these individuals, as documented in Scripture, provide us with profound insights into how we can understand and embrace our own calling.

Noah's Faithful Response
Genesis 6:13-22

Noah's story is a powerful example of obedience and faith amidst adversity. When God instructed Noah to build an ark in preparation for a catastrophic flood, Noah obeyed without hesitation, even though the command seemed illogical and unprecedented. While likely facing skepticism and mockery from others, Noah's unwavering faith and trust in God's word serve as a compelling reminder for us to trust and act on God's instructions, even when they seem to defy conventional wisdom or understanding.

Moses' Reluctant Leadership
Exodus 3:10-12

Moses' initial reluctance to accept God's call to lead the Israelites out of Egypt is a narrative many can relate to. He felt inadequate and questioned his ability to fulfill such a monumental task. However, Moses' journey from reluctance to becoming a pivotal leader is a testament to God's faithfulness in equipping those He calls. Moses' life reassures us that our ability to fulfill our commission depends not on our own strength but on God's power working through us.

Esther's Courage for Advocacy
Esther 4:14

Esther's story is a striking example of courage and advocacy. Faced with a life-threatening decision to approach the king unbidden – a move that could have led to her death – to save her people from genocide, Esther displayed remarkable bravery. Her resolve to act for the greater good, encapsulated in her words, *"If I perish, I perish,"* highlights the courage sometimes required in fulfilling our commission, especially when it involves standing against injustice and risking personal safety.

Paul's Missionary Zeal
Acts 9:15-16

The transformation of Saul to Paul is one of the most dramatic narratives in the New Testament. His conversion and subsequent missionary journeys, as detailed in the Book of Acts, showcase the radical change and far-reaching impact that can occur when we wholeheartedly embrace God's commission. Paul's life is an inspiring example of dedication, zeal, and the transformative power of a life committed to God's call.

David's Heart for God
Psalm 51:10-12

David's journey from a shepherd boy to the king of Israel illustrates the importance of having a heart aligned with God. Despite his flaws and sins, David's deep desire for repentance and his pursuit of a relationship with God is evident throughout the Psalms. His plea for a clean heart in Psalm 51 reveals a profound understanding of repentance, devotion, and the need for God's guidance and presence.

As you reflect on these biblical accounts and their related scriptures, consider how they can inform and inspire your own journey. What lessons can you draw from their experiences of faith, obedience, courage, transformation, and repentance? How do these stories resonate with your personal commission and the path that God is calling you to walk?

Each of these figures faced unique challenges and opportunities as they pursued their divine commissions. Their stories encourage us to remain faithful, to trust in God's plan, and to be willing to step out in faith, even when the path ahead is uncertain.

In understanding our divine commission, it's crucial to recognize that God's calling is often interwoven with our life experiences, our strengths, and sometimes even our weaknesses. Just as God used Moses' background, Esther's position, and Paul's zeal for His purposes, He can use every aspect of our lives for His glory.

Moreover, these examples remind us that fulfilling our divine commission is not a solitary endeavor. Each of these biblical figures had relationships and communities that played a crucial role in their journeys. Similarly, we are called to engage with our communities, churches, and fellow believers as we pursue our calling.

Thus, let's further explore divine commission with an open heart, ready to learn from the examples set before us in Scripture. Let's be inspired by their faith, encouraged by their perseverance, and motivated by their devotion to God's call. As we consider their stories, let's reflect on how we can apply these lessons to our own lives, embracing our unique calling with faith, courage, and a commitment to follow wherever God leads us.

FINDING STRENGTH

In the final section of the chapter, we address a critical element of living out our divine commission: perseverance through challenges. The path God sets before us often includes trials and obstacles. Yet, these difficulties are not mere impediments; they serve as opportunities for deepening our reliance on Him.

Embracing Trials with Joy
James 1:2-4

The Apostle James implores us to consider trials as occasions for joy, knowing that they foster perseverance. This perspective is vital when encountering challenges in fulfilling our commission. Recognizing that trials refine and fortify our faith allows us to meet them with resilience and determination.

Joseph's Resilience
Genesis 50:20

The story of Joseph powerfully illustrates perseverance and faith. Despite facing betrayal, slavery, and unjust imprisonment, Joseph remained steadfast in his faith. His reflection, "*You intended to harm me, but God intended it for good,*" showcases how God can transform even the gravest circumstances into vehicles for His purpose.

Peter's Restoration
John 21:15-19

After his denial of Christ, Peter confronted a profound personal crisis. His subsequent restoration by Jesus exemplifies the idea that our failures are not final. Instead, they can signify the start of a renewed commitment to our divine commission, enriched by our experiences.

Paul's Endurance
2 Corinthians 4:8-9

The ministry of Paul was riddled with hardships, yet he persisted unwaveringly. His words, "*We are hard-pressed on every side, but not crushed,*" embody the resilience required to continue God's work despite facing adversity.

Finding Strength in Christ
Philippians 4:13

During challenging times, our strength is derived from Christ. Paul's affirmation, "*I can do all this through Him who gives me strength,*" serves as a powerful reminder that through Christ, we are equipped to surmount any challenge.

As you contemplate these scriptural examples, reflect on the challenges you encounter in your own journey of divine commission. How can these lessons of perseverance, reliance on God, and the transformative nature of trials guide and bolster you?

Embracing your divine commission with perseverance is a demonstration of resilient faith. It involves recognizing that each challenge is an integral part of fulfilling God's purpose for your life. So, be inspired to view trials not as setbacks but as catalysts for growth and a deeper commitment to your calling.

The journey of fulfilling one's divine commission is often marked by moments of uncertainty and testing. These moments, while difficult, are instrumental in shaping us into more effective servants and representatives of God's kingdom. They teach us patience, humility, and reliance on God's strength rather than our own.

Moreover, these challenges often bring us closer to God. In our moments of struggle, we are compelled to seek Him more earnestly, delve deeper into His Word, and rely more fully on His guidance and providence.

Through this process, we develop a more intimate relationship with God, understanding His character and ways more deeply.

The stories of biblical figures like Joseph, Peter, and Paul also teach us the value of perspective. They remind us that God's view of our situations often differs from our own. What may seem like an insurmountable obstacle can be an opportunity for God to demonstrate His power and faithfulness.

Furthermore, these challenges equip us to minister to others. Through our experiences, we gain empathy and understanding for others facing similar trials. We become better equipped to offer support, guidance, and encouragement, fulfilling our commission to be bearers of God's love and compassion.

Let's approach challenges with faith, resilience, and a willingness to learn and grow. Let's trust that God is with us, refining us and using every situation for our good and His glory. As we face trials, let's hold fast to the promises of God, drawing strength from His Word and presence and moving forward with confidence in the role He has called us to play in His grand narrative.

OUR SPIRITUAL LIFE
SHOULD *Permeate*
ALL AREAS OF OUR
EXISTENCE.

CHAPTER SEVEN

THE RESPONSIBILITIES OF A SON

Let us delve into the challenge of balancing our spiritual duties with our earthly responsibilities. This task is crucial for our well-being and is fundamental to how effectively we live out our calling as children of God. This balance is a delicate dance between the spiritual and the secular, requiring careful navigation and constant vigilance.

In the life of a believer, balancing spiritual life with earthly commitments is a common yet complex challenge. We find ourselves juggling the demands of work, family, and personal ambitions with our commitment to prayer, worship, and spiritual growth. This act of juggling is not just necessary for maintaining a holistic Christian life; it is essential for ensuring that our earthly existence is in harmony with our spiritual identity.

The Bible offers us profound guidance on achieving this balance. Jesus' teaching in Matthew 6:33, where He advises seeking God's kingdom and righteousness first, is pivotal. This directive helps us prioritize our daily lives, aligning them with God's will. It suggests that our spiritual responsibilities should not be an add-on to our lives but the lens through which we view all our earthly roles and activities.

Looking at biblical figures like Daniel and Esther, we learn valuable lessons in balancing our secular responsibilities with our spiritual commitments. Despite holding prominent positions in foreign lands, these figures remained unwavering in their faith, skillfully navigating their earthly duties without compromising their devotion to God. Their lives are powerful examples of how to live out our faith in environments that may not always be conducive to spiritual practices.

In practical terms, finding this balance can involve setting aside specific times for prayer and Bible study, even amidst a busy schedule. It may also mean making decisions in our workplace or family life that reflect our commitment to our faith. It's about ensuring that our faith is not compartmentalized but integrated into every aspect of our daily existence.

Achieving this balance often requires seeking wisdom and support. This guidance can come from personal prayer, fellowship with other believers, and the insights of spiritual mentors. Such counsel can be invaluable in navigating the complexities of a life that strives to honor God in all things.

However, this journey of balancing our spiritual and earthly duties is ongoing. It necessitates continual adjustment and reevaluation as life's circumstances change. Yet, with a heart and mind focused on God, we can successfully navigate this path, fulfilling our earthly responsibilities and spiritual calling.

In navigating these dual roles, we must recognize that our spiritual life should permeate all areas of our existence. Our faith is not just for Sundays or quiet moments of prayer; it's for the workplace, the home, and every interaction we have. Whether in mundane tasks or significant decisions, our actions should reflect our commitment to God and His principles.

Furthermore, achieving this balance is not about dividing our time equally between spiritual and secular activities but about ensuring that our faith informs and enhances every part of our lives. It's recognizing that our everyday activities are opportunities to live out our faith, no matter how secular they may seem.

Discerning the seasons of life is also crucial in this balancing act. There are times when our spiritual commitments may need to take precedence and other times when our earthly responsibilities require more focus. Understanding and responding appropriately to these seasons is key to maintaining a healthy balance.

Embracing this duality also involves acknowledging the value and significance of our earthly roles as part of God's plan. Our professional, familial, and community roles are not just secular obligations but opportunities to demonstrate God's love and grace. They are ministries in their own right, avenues through which we can live out our faith in practical, tangible ways. In this chapter, let us approach the challenge of balancing our spiritual and earthly duties with wisdom, prayer, and a heart open to God's guidance. Let's strive to integrate our faith into every aspect of our lives, recognizing that every moment is an opportunity to serve God and fulfill our divine calling. As we navigate this journey, let's be encouraged by the assurance that with God's help, we can find harmony in our dual roles and live out our responsibilities as sons of God in a faithful and effective way.

THE RESPONSIBILITY OF REPRESENTATION

Here, we focus on the profound responsibility that we bear as God's children: to represent His character and essence in our daily lives. This role goes beyond mere verbal proclamation of our faith; it's about being a living testament to God's love, grace, and truth in a world that desperately needs to encounter His reflection.

As believers, we are called to be ambassadors for Christ, a concept eloquently expressed in 2 Corinthians 5:20. This ambassadorship is a holistic role, encompassing much more than just words. It demands that we embody the principles and virtues of the kingdom of God in every facet of our lives, making the love, kindness, and righteousness of God tangible and visible through our actions and interactions. True representation of God requires more than surface-level expressions of faith. It calls for a deep introspection of our hearts and lives, ensuring that our values, decisions, and lifestyles align with the teachings of Jesus. This call to authenticity means that our inner spiritual life should consistently resonate with our outward actions.

At the heart of our representation is love – a love that mirrors God's profound love for us. As emphasized in 1 John 4:7-8, loving others is not merely a commandment but an intrinsic characteristic of those who know God. Our love for others, manifested in various forms, becomes a potent demonstration of our Heavenly Father's love.

Representing God in a complex world that often presents contradictory values can be challenging. It necessitates wisdom to navigate situations where our faith and values might be put to the test. It involves maintaining our integrity in our beliefs while extending grace and understanding to those who may hold different perspectives.

Embracing this responsibility of representation is a continuous journey of learning and growth. It involves regularly examining ourselves, seeking God's guidance, and being receptive to correction and change. It's about advancing in spiritual maturity and comprehension so that our portrayal of God becomes more lucid and influential.

As you engage with this section, take a moment to reflect on how you represent God in your own life. Consider areas where your actions and words could more accurately mirror God's character. How can you deepen your capacity for love, grace, and truth to become a more effective ambassador for Christ? Living as God's ambassadors also means knowing how our actions and words impact those around us. It's about being mindful that we are often the only 'Bible' some people will read. Therefore, our conduct should not only reflect our faith but should also invite others to experience the love and grace of God.

Furthermore, this responsibility extends to how we handle conflicts, challenges, and even misunderstandings. It's about exhibiting qualities such as forgiveness, patience, and humility, which are hallmarks of Christ's character. In doing so, we not only represent God but also foster environments where His love can flourish.

Throughout this chapter, let us move forward with a heart committed to authenticity and growth. Let's strive to embody God's character in all we do, being mindful that we are His representatives in this world. As we navigate this journey, let's continually seek God's wisdom and guidance to grow in our ability to reflect His image accurately and lovingly. Let's embrace the call to be ambassadors for Christ, representing Him in a way that draws others closer to His transformative love and grace.

LEARNING RESPONSIBILITY

Delving deeper into the topic of this chapter, we focus on the vital aspect of cultivating spiritual maturity. This journey is not merely about reveling in the privileges of sonship but also about embracing the growth and maturity that accompany our spiritual responsibilities. It's a path that involves understanding the significance of our role as God's children and learning to live in a way that reflects the weight of this responsibility.

The Bible emphasizes the importance of responsibility in our spiritual walk. Jesus' words in Luke 12:48 remind us that significant responsibilities come with the great blessings we receive. As recipients of God's grace and love, we are called to live lives that honor these gifts. This involves stewarding our blessings wisely and committing to a lifestyle that aligns with godly principles.

We can look to the early church, depicted in Acts 2:42-47, as a model of collective responsibility. Their dedication to teaching, fellowship, prayer, and communal sharing demonstrates that responsibility is not an individual pursuit alone but a communal one. Their example shows us how living in a community and sharing our lives with fellow believers is integral to our spiritual growth and maturity.

Timothy's example, under Paul's mentorship, highlights the potential of young believers who embrace their responsibilities. Paul's exhortation to Timothy in 1 Timothy 4:12 to set an example in speech, conduct, love, faith, and purity is a call to all believers, regardless of age or maturity, to live in a manner that honors our calling as God's children. The Parable of the Talents in Matthew 25:14-30 teaches us about stewardship of our spiritual gifts. This parable is a clarion call to use our talents and resources not just for our personal benefit but for the advancement of God's kingdom. It's a reminder that we are accountable for utilizing the gifts God has entrusted us.

Growth in responsibility is often accompanied by discipline. As Hebrews 12:11 indicates, discipline from the Lord, though challenging, ultimately produces a harvest of righteousness and peace. Engaging in regular spiritual practices like prayer and Bible study is not just routine; these are vital disciplines that foster growth, maturity, and a deeper understanding of God's will.

Our role in the community of believers is also crucial to our maturity. The directive in Galatians 6:2 to bear one another's burdens underlines that maturity includes supporting, caring, and being present for our fellow Christians. It's about being an active, contributing member of the body of Christ, where our growth benefits us and those around us.

As you ponder this section, reflect on your journey of growing in spiritual responsibility. Ask yourself where you need further development and how you can more effectively steward the gifts and opportunities God has provided you. Are there areas in your life where more discipline or commitment is needed? How can you engage more deeply with the community of believers to enhance your growth and contribute to theirs?

This journey of learning responsibility is an ongoing process toward spiritual maturity. It's about continually seeking to align our lives more closely with God's will, to grow in our understanding of His word, and to live out our faith in tangible, impactful ways. It's a path marked by a commitment to personal development, a dedication to community, and a steadfast focus on fulfilling God's purpose for our lives.

Let's embrace the call to maturity with dedication and zeal. Let's commit to growing in every aspect of our spiritual lives, recognizing that each step we take in maturing as God's children is a step toward fulfilling the incredible plan He has for each of us. Let's approach this path with a heart open to learning, a spirit ready for transformation, and a willingness to embrace all the responsibilities that come with being a child of God.

SERVING AND LEADING: The Dual Role of a Son

In the final section of this chapter, we explore the integral dual role of a son in God's kingdom: serving and leading. These aspects, far from being separate or contradictory, are deeply interconnected and form the core of our spiritual journey. Each aspect, serving and leading, enhances and informs the other, creating a dynamic and holistic approach to our Christian walk.

The concept of the servant-leader, exemplified by Jesus Christ, is at the heart of this discussion. Jesus embodied this role perfectly, demonstrating that true leadership is fundamentally rooted in service. This fact is vividly illustrated in John 13:14-15, where, after washing His disciples' feet, Jesus encourages them to follow His example of humble service. This act is not just a lesson in humility; it's a powerful directive about the nature of true leadership – leading by example, serving with humility, and prioritizing the needs of others.

Service is a foundational element of our Christian life. It involves putting others' needs ahead of our own and reflecting God's love and compassion through our actions. Far from being a sign of weakness, service is a testament to strength, character, and commitment. It is often through acts of service that we encounter significant opportunities for spiritual growth, influencing others, and developing leadership qualities.

In the context of being a son of God, leadership is about more than just holding a position or title. It's about guiding, inspiring, and nurturing others in their faith journey. It involves being a positive and godly influence in the lives of those around us – our families, communities, or workplaces. Christian leadership is characterized by qualities like integrity, humility, and a firm commitment to living out God's principles.

Balancing the roles of service and leadership requires deep understanding and discernment of God's calling for our lives. It involves wisdom to recognize when to take the initiative to lead and when to step back and serve. This balance is critical for effective ministry and making a meaningful impact in the kingdom of God.

Growth in both service and leadership is an ongoing journey that involves continuous learning, self-reflection, and actively seeking God's guidance. It's about being open to the challenges and opportunities God places before us and responding with a heart ready to serve and lead. This growth process is not always linear or straightforward; it often involves navigating complex situations and making tough decisions that test our commitment to these dual roles.

As you reflect on this section, consider how you currently embody these roles of serving and leading in your life. Are there areas where you need further development or growth? How can you more effectively model the servant-leader archetype that Jesus so perfectly exemplified? Reflect on how you can expand your capacity to serve others and lead by example, keeping in mind the humility and selflessness that should characterize these efforts.

Embracing the call to serve and lead is critical to fulfilling our responsibilities as sons in God's kingdom. It's about recognizing that through these roles, we are not just fulfilling personal ambitions or goals but actively participating in God's work and furthering His kingdom on earth.

Let's commit to embracing both service and leadership as integral parts of our identity as children of God as we navigate our spiritual journey. Let's strive to exemplify the servant-leader model in all aspects of our lives, understanding that through this dual role, we are called to make a significant impact in the lives of others and the world. Let's approach this calling with humility, courage, and a willingness to grow, knowing that in doing so, we are living out our true purpose and responsibility as sons of the Most High.

This journey of embracing both serving and leading is not only about impacting others but also about personal transformation. As we serve, we learn empathy, selflessness, and compassion. As we lead, we develop wisdom, courage, and integrity. These roles, therefore, are not just responsibilities we carry out but are pathways to becoming more like Christ, who perfectly embodied both servant and leader.

Furthermore, our commitment to serving and leading should permeate all areas of our lives. In our families, we are called to serve and lead with love and patience. In our workplaces, we can demonstrate integrity and influence others positively. In our communities and churches, we can serve those in need and lead in various capacities, contributing to the well-being and growth of those around us.

It's also important to recognize that we will encounter challenges in both serving and leading. Serving may sometimes mean putting others' needs above our own, which can be demanding. Leading might involve making tough decisions or guiding others through difficult situations. Our character is refined in these moments, and our reliance on God deepens.

In embracing the dual roles of serving and leading, it is crucial to remain grounded in God's Word and prayer. These practices provide the wisdom, strength, and guidance needed to navigate the complexities of these roles. They keep us connected to our ultimate leader, Jesus Christ, and align our actions with His will.

As we reflect on this section, we must consider practical ways to cultivate these roles in our daily lives. This might involve volunteering for service opportunities, taking on leadership roles in our church or community, or simply being more intentional about serving and leading in our existing relationships and spheres of influence.

In serving, let's look for practical, tangible ways to demonstrate Christ's love. In leading, let's seek to inspire, encourage, and guide others toward God's truth. In both, let's be examples of the grace and mercy we have received from God.

Let's embrace our dual role as servant-leaders with enthusiasm and commitment. Let's see every act of service and every opportunity to lead as a chance to glorify God, grow in our faith, and impact the world for His kingdom. By embodying these roles, we live out the fullness of our calling as children of God, reflecting His character and love in a world that needs it more than ever. Let's embark on this journey with open hearts, ready to serve and lead in the unique ways God has equipped and called each of us.

CHALLENGES FORTIFY OUR FAITH AND STRENGTHEN OUR CHARACTER.

CHAPTER EIGHT

THE CHALLENGES OF SONSHIP

At the start of this chapter, our attention is drawn to the external challenges we encounter as children of God. Living in a world that often operates counter to God's principles presents a unique set of trials and tests for believers. These challenges require us to navigate a path that remains true to our faith while engaging with a world that frequently conflicts with our Christian values.

One of the most significant external challenges is the pressure to conform to societal norms and values that contradict Christian beliefs. This pressure can manifest in various forms, from subtle influences in media and entertainment to more direct pressures in our workplaces or social circles. Romans 12:2 advises us not to conform to the pattern of this world but to be transformed by the renewing of our minds. This scripture is a powerful reminder that our values and decisions should be shaped by our faith and the teachings of Scripture, not by the prevailing cultural trends or societal expectations. For many believers, especially in certain regions and communities, following Christ involves facing persecution and opposition. Jesus' warning in John 15:18—that if the world hated Him, it would hate His followers too—is a stark reminder of this reality. This aspect of sonship calls for courage, steadfastness, and a deep commitment to our faith, even in the face of hostility and discrimination.

In today's age of information overload, discerning truth from deception becomes increasingly difficult. The challenge lies in navigating misinformation, half-truths, and deceptive narratives that pervade our media and social networks. 2 Timothy 3:16-17 teaches us about the reliability and authority of Scripture as a guide in a world where truth can often be obscured or twisted. This guidance is crucial for believers to navigate the complexities of the modern world with wisdom and discernment.

Engaging with the world while maintaining our distinct Christian identity is a delicate balance. The call to be in the world but not of it, as described in John 17:15-16, involves actively participating in society and serving others while upholding our Christian values and ethics. This balance requires us to be both salt and light—preserving our faith and values while shining God's truth and love into the world around us.

As followers of Christ, we may also face criticism and judgment from those who do not understand or accept our beliefs. This criticism or judgment can come in the form of dismissive attitudes, hostile opposition, or even well-intentioned but misguided advice from those close to us. Responding to such criticism with grace and truth, as modeled by Jesus, is a vital skill in navigating these challenges. It involves a combination of firmness in our convictions and a loving, compassionate approach to those who oppose or misunderstand us.

In facing these external challenges, the role of prayer and the support of a Christian community cannot be overstated. Prayer is our direct line to God for strength, guidance, and comfort. The support of a faith community provides a network of encouragement, advice, and fellowship, which is essential for standing firm in our faith amidst external pressures.

As you contemplate this section, reflect on the external challenges you encounter in your own walk of faith. Consider how you can apply biblical principles to effectively navigate these challenges. These trials are not mere obstacles but opportunities to grow in faith, resilience, and commitment as a son of God. They can deepen our reliance on God, strengthen our character, and enhance our witness to the world.

Navigating these external challenges is an ongoing process. It involves constant vigilance, a commitment to continually growing in our understanding of God's Word, and an openness to the Holy Spirit's guidance. It's about learning to discern the times and knowing how to respond in a way that honors God while also effectively engaging with the world around us.

In looking at the challenges of sonship in this chapter, let's do so with an attitude of faith and perseverance. Let's be encouraged by the knowledge that these challenges are part of our journey as God's children and that He equips and accompanies us through each one. Let's embrace these challenges as opportunities to demonstrate our faith, grow in our relationship with God, and effectively witness His grace and truth in a fallen world. Let's navigate these external challenges with wisdom, grace, and a steadfast commitment to living out our identity as sons of the Most High.

THE BATTLE WITHIN

Navigating the internal struggles that often accompany our journey as children of God is an integral focus of this chapter. These internal battles, which take place within the landscapes of our minds and hearts, are sometimes as formidable as any external challenge we might face. Understanding and addressing these hidden fronts of sonship is crucial for our spiritual growth and resilience.

Wrestling with doubts and questions of faith is a common experience among believers. It is a natural part of our spiritual journey to question and seek deeper understanding. The Gospel of Mark recounts a father's desperate plea, "*I do believe; help me overcome my unbelief!*" (Mark 9:24). This poignant moment captures the essence of our internal struggles with faith. It reminds us that bringing our uncertainties to God is okay, seeking His guidance, clarity, and reassurance.

Many of us can resonate with Paul's candid reflection in Romans 7:15-25 about his internal conflict with sin. This struggle against sin and temptation highlights our ongoing need for God's grace. It also underscores the importance of cultivating spiritual vigilance and continually striving to align our actions with our renewed nature in Christ.

Maintaining consistent spiritual disciplines, such as prayer and Bible study, can often be challenging. The demands of daily life and various distractions can make it difficult to prioritize these spiritual practices. However, they are crucial for nurturing our relationship with God and providing strength and guidance in our internal battles.

Acknowledging and confronting our personal weaknesses and vulnerabilities is another aspect of our internal struggle. Paul's experience, where he speaks of boasting in his weaknesses because Christ's power is made perfect in them (2 Corinthians 12:9-10), offers a transformative perspective on how we view and handle our vulnerabilities. It encourages us to rely not on our strength but on God's power working through our weaknesses.

Emotional turmoil, involving complex emotions like fear, loneliness, or anxiety, is also part of our internal journey. The Psalms offer profound insights into managing these emotions. For instance, Psalm 42:11

shows a heartfelt process of self-reflection and finding hope in God amidst emotional challenges. It teaches us to honestly express our emotions before God and to find comfort in His presence and promises.

The role of a supportive Christian community in navigating these internal challenges cannot be overstated. Fellow believers provide encouragement, prayer, and wise counsel. They help us stay grounded in our faith and offer perspectives that can guide us through our internal battles.

As you contemplate the internal struggles that accompany your spiritual journey, think about ways to actively engage with these challenges. Consider how you can use them as opportunities for growth, character development, and deepening your reliance on God. Reflect on the importance of being transparent with God about your struggles, seeking His wisdom in Scripture, and engaging in honest prayer.

Additionally, don't underestimate the value of sharing your struggles with trusted members of your faith community. They can often provide support, accountability, and wisdom that help you navigate these challenges more effectively.

In conclusion, as we explore the internal struggles inherent in the challenges of sonship, let's do so with a commitment to growth and a reliance on God's strength. Let's view these struggles as opportunities to deepen our faith, enhance our understanding, and grow closer to God. By acknowledging and confronting these challenges head-on, we can cultivate inner strength and resilience that equip us to fulfill our calling as children of God. Let's embark on this journey with a spirit of perseverance, openness to God's transforming work within us, and a willingness to lean on our community for support and guidance.

OVERCOMING ADVERSITY

In our journey of sonship, we arrive at a crucial aspect of our spiritual development: building resilience through overcoming adversity. Trials and challenges, though often difficult, are instrumental in fortifying our faith and shaping our character. These experiences, while they may seem daunting, are vital opportunities for growth and strengthening.

The Bible, particularly in James 1:2-4, encourages us to view trials as opportunities for joy, as they test our faith and foster perseverance. This perspective is essential in building resilience. Recognizing trials as opportunities rather than mere obstacles allows us to grow in faith and strength. It's about learning to see the hand of God at work in our difficulties, using them to refine and develop us.

Job's story is an exemplary model of enduring severe trials while maintaining faith in God. Despite experiencing immense suffering, Job's resilience and steadfastness (Job 1:20-22) exemplify the depth of trust and perseverance that can be developed through adversity. Job's journey teaches us about the unshakeable nature of faith that endures despite overwhelming challenges.

King David, through his numerous adversities, provides another powerful example. His Psalms are candid reflections of his struggles, yet they consistently reveal his unwavering faith in God. David's habit of turning to God in prayer and trust during his most challenging times shows us the importance of seeking God's presence and comfort in our trials.

The Apostle Paul's perspective on suffering, as illustrated in 2 Corinthians 4:8-9, highlights how hardships can be a means to demonstrate God's power and grace. Despite facing various difficulties, Paul's resilience showcases the strength that comes from a reliance on God. His approach teaches us to view our sufferings as opportunities for God's power to be displayed in our lives.

Building resilience is more than enduring trials; it's about actively seeking to understand God's purpose in them and learning from them. It's about developing a spirit of endurance that actively engages with challenges, trusting that God is using these experiences to mold us into stronger, more faithful believers. This growth in resilience is not just for our benefit but also equips us to support and encourage others in their trials.

The support of a Christian community is invaluable in this process. Fellow believers provide encouragement, wisdom, and practical help, reinforcing the notion that we are not alone in our struggles. The community reminds us of our collective strength in Christ and the shared journey of faith we embark upon.

While engaging in this section, reflect on the adversities you have faced or are currently facing. Consider how these challenges can be catalysts for strengthening your faith and resilience. Embrace these trials as opportunities for growth, trusting that God is working to build endurance, character, and hope in you through them.

Overcoming adversity and building resilience is a continuous process. It involves learning to trust God's sovereignty, embracing His refining work, and finding strength in His promises. It's about learning to lean not on our understanding but on His unending grace and wisdom.

As we navigate the challenges of sonship and the adversities that come with it, let's approach them with faith, perseverance, and an open heart. Let's view these trials as opportunities to strengthen our faith, deepen our trust in God, and become more resilient and mature believers. Let's embrace the journey of overcoming adversity, knowing that in each challenge lies an opportunity for growth and a deeper experience of God's faithfulness.

RESPONDING TO CHALLENGES

In the last section of this chapter, we delve into the crucial aspect of responding to the challenges of sonship with faith and wisdom. This process is not merely about enduring difficulties but actively engaging with them in a manner that promotes spiritual growth and deepens our understanding. It's about harnessing these challenges as opportunities to strengthen our faith and cultivate wisdom.

Faith serves as our steadfast anchor amidst life's tumultuous storms. Hebrews 11:1 eloquently defines faith as having confidence in what we hope for and assurance about what we do not see. In the face of challenges, it's our faith that keeps us grounded, reminding us of God's unchanging promises and His ever-present guidance, even when our circumstances seem daunting or the path ahead appears uncertain.

James 1:5 encourages us to seek wisdom from God, particularly in times of trial. Wisdom equips us to navigate complex situations with discernment, understanding, and a perspective that transcends immediate circumstances. It allows us to recognize God's broader plan and purposes at work, even amidst adversity.

The responses of Jesus to various challenges during His ministry provide a profound model for us. Whether it was overcoming temptation in the wilderness (Matthew 4:1-11) or handling opposition from religious leaders, Jesus consistently responded with wisdom and discernment, grounded in Scripture and aligned with His Father's will. His example teaches us to respond to our challenges by focusing on God's truth and purposes.

Prayer is our powerful tool in navigating challenges. As Paul suggests in Philippians 4:6-7, presenting our requests to God with thanksgiving brings about a peace that surpasses understanding and guards our hearts and minds. In prayer, we find the strength, guidance, and peace necessary to face trials with a calm and steady spirit.

Responding to challenges also involves a delicate balance between taking action and trusting in God. It's about doing our part – seeking counsel, making informed decisions, and taking steps towards resolution – while simultaneously trusting in God's overarching control and perfect timing. This balance is crucial for effective problem-solving and maintaining a peace that comes from faith.

The support of a Christian community is invaluable in facing challenges. Fellow believers offer shared experiences, encouragement, and prayerful support, providing the strength and perspective needed to navigate difficult times. This communal support reminds us that we are not alone in our struggles and that the body of Christ is designed to uphold and strengthen its members.

So, consider how you currently respond to challenges in your life. Are you leaning into these difficulties with faith and wisdom? How can you more effectively use these trials as opportunities for growth? Embrace each challenge as an opportunity to demonstrate courageous faith, grow in wisdom, and develop a deeper spiritual maturity. Each challenge we face is an opportunity to trust God more deeply and to develop character traits that align us more closely with Christ. It's an invitation to grow in faith, learn patience, practice humility, and cultivate a heart that seeks God in all circumstances.

As we navigate the challenges of sonship, let's do so with a perspective that views each difficulty as a stepping stone towards greater faith and deeper wisdom. Let's approach these challenges with a heart willing to learn, change, and grow, trusting that God is using each situation to shape us into the image of His Son. Let's respond to our challenges with the assurance that God is with us, guiding us through each trial and equipping us with everything we need to overcome.

CHAPTER NINE

SOBRIETY: THE TRUTH ABOUT SONSHIP

In this chapter, our primary focus is on dispelling common myths and misconceptions about what it truly means to be a son of God. In today's world, with its multitude of interpretations and teachings, it is crucial to cultivate a clear and biblically grounded understanding of sonship. This endeavor is about separating fact from fiction and embracing the true essence of our identity in Christ.

A prevalent misconception is that sonship in God's kingdom is exclusively about privileges. While being a child of God indeed comes with incredible blessings, it also encompasses responsibilities, opportunities for personal growth, and, at times, enduring suffering for righteousness' sake (Romans 8:17). This more comprehensive understanding of sonship paints a picture of a journey that is rich and rewarding, yet also challenging and transformative.

Another common myth is that sonship is primarily tied to biological lineage or belonging to a particular group. However, the teachings of Galatians 3:26-28 clarify that in Christ, we all are God's children through faith. This spiritual kinship transcends physical descent, cultural backgrounds, and social statuses, uniting diverse individuals under a common identity in Christ.

There is also a misconception that we can earn our status as God's children through good deeds or moral behavior. However, Ephesians 2:8-9 categorically states that our sonship is a gift of grace, not a result of our works, thereby nullifying any grounds for boasting. This understanding emphasizes that our relationship with God is rooted in His unmerited favor, not in our ability to earn His approval.

Often overlooked is the role of discipline within the context of sonship. Hebrews 12:7-11 elucidates that God's discipline is a manifestation of His love and is integral to our growth and sharing in His holiness. Although sometimes challenging, this discipline is essential for our spiritual development and alignment with God's character.

The belief that being a child of God equates to a life free from hardship is misleading. Jesus Himself cautioned about the inevitability of trials in this world (John 16:33), but He also promised His peace and the assurance of His overcoming power. This reality invites us to find strength and comfort in Him, even amid adversity.

Furthermore, sonship is not a static state but a dynamic and ongoing relationship with God. It encompasses daily growth, continual learning, and a journey of progressively becoming more like Christ. This aspect of sonship highlights the evolving nature of our relationship with God, marked by constant change and maturity.

Throughout this section, take time to reflect on your own understanding of sonship. Are there any misconceptions or limited views you've held that need reevaluation? Embracing the true essence of sonship, as revealed in Scripture, invites you to experience the fullness and richness of what it means to be a child of God. It's about understanding the balance of privilege and responsibility, grace and discipline, comfort and challenge that characterizes our journey as God's children.

This journey of sonship is not merely about enjoying the benefits of a relationship with God but also about actively participating in His kingdom work. It involves embracing both the joys and the trials that come with being a child of God, finding in each an opportunity for growth and deeper connection with Him.

While we explore the truths about sonship in this chapter, let's do so with open hearts and minds, ready to embrace the full spectrum of what this identity entails. Let's seek to understand and live out our sonship in a way that is grounded in biblical truth, marked by a commitment to spiritual growth, and characterized by a deep, enduring relationship with our Heavenly Father. Let's journey through this exploration with a desire to grow closer to God, deepen our understanding of His love and purpose for us, and live out our identity as His children with faith, wisdom, and authenticity.

THE RESPONSIBILITY OF FREEDOM

There is a profound responsibility that accompanies the freedom we enjoy as children of God. This freedom, a gift of immeasurable value, is not just a license for personal liberty but carries with it a significant obligation to live a life that reflects God's purpose and will.

The freedom we receive as God's children is meant to be a tool for righteousness. Galatians 5:13 urges us to use our liberty not as an opportunity for self-indulgence but as a means to serve others in love. This perspective on freedom challenges us to employ our newfound liberty in Christ to foster righteousness, compassion, and justice. It's about reflecting God's character in our actions, using our freedom to impact those around us positively and advance the cause of God's kingdom.

However, this freedom can be easily misused. As Paul warns in Romans 6:1-2, our freedom in Christ should not be construed as permission to continue in sin. This misuse of freedom is a pitfall that every believer must conscientiously avoid. Our new life in Christ calls us to higher standards of conduct, to a life that is in line with the transformation we have experienced through His grace. The call to holy living, as highlighted in 1 Peter

1:15-16, is an integral aspect of our freedom. Being holy in all our conduct, just as God is holy, is a mandate that comes with our identity as His children. This call to holiness challenges us to live lives that are distinct from the world, lives that are pleasing and honorable to God.

Our freedom in Christ also involves making decisions that honor God. It's about exercising discernment in our daily choices, ensuring that our actions align with God's principles and purposes. The Holy Spirit guides this decision-making process, providing wisdom and direction as we navigate the complexities of life with our newfound freedom.

The role of the Holy Spirit in guiding our freedom cannot be overstated. As stated in Romans 8:14, those led by the Spirit of God are indeed His children. The Spirit's guidance is crucial in helping us to navigate our freedom responsibly, steering us away from selfish desires and towards God's greater purposes.

Ultimately, our freedom as sons of God is a call to embrace responsibility. It's about recognizing the wider implications of our actions and choices, not just for ourselves but for others and for the mission of God's kingdom. Our freedom is an opportunity to live out the values of the kingdom, be ambassadors of Christ, and positively influence the world around us.

Now, reflect on how you are exercising your freedom in Christ. Are your life choices and daily actions a reflection of God's character and will? Are you using your freedom to serve, uplift, and advance the cause of righteousness? Embrace the responsibility that comes with your freedom, letting it guide you to live a life filled with purpose, service, and a deep commitment to the values of God's kingdom.

This freedom is a precious gift, one that offers us the opportunity to live in a truly liberating way. It allows us to break free from the shackles of sin and embrace a life that is rich in meaning and purpose. However, with this gift comes the challenge to live in a way that honors God and advances His purposes in the world.

We should explore this section of Chapter 9 with a heart that is eager to embrace the fullness of our freedom in Christ. Let's strive to live lives that are marked by righteousness, service, and a deep commitment to God's will. Let's use our freedom as a tool for positive change, as a means to demonstrate the love and grace of God, and as an opportunity to grow in holiness and spiritual maturity. Let's live with purposeful freedom, embracing the responsibility that comes with our identity as children of God and using our liberty to make a meaningful impact in our world.

WALKING IN AUTHORITY

An authority accompanies our identity as children of God. This authority, a significant aspect of our sonship, is essential for effectively living out our calling. Understanding and walking in this authority allows us to operate in alignment with God's purposes and make a meaningful impact in our world.

Our authority as God's children is deeply rooted in our identity in Christ. Romans 8:15-17 illuminates this truth, revealing that we are not merely servants but children of God, and as such, we are heirs – heirs of God and co-heirs with Christ. This heirship bestows upon us an authority that goes beyond human understanding – an authority to act in alignment with God's will, to make decisions that reflect His kingdom, and to bring about His purposes on earth.

However, exercising this authority requires humility and love. Jesus Christ, our ultimate example, demonstrated how to wield authority not for personal gain but in service to others and for the glory of God. Philippians 2:5-8 encourages us to adopt the same mindset as Christ, who, despite His divinity, chose the path of humility and obedience. We are called to use our authority in a manner that serves, uplifts, and honors God, reflecting Christ's character in our actions.

As believers, we are also endowed with authority over spiritual forces of evil. Ephesians 6:10-12 reminds us of the spiritual battle we are engaged in and the authority we possess in Christ to stand against these forces. This authority equips us to confront and overcome spiritual challenges, not in our strength but through the power and authority of Christ within us.

Prayer is a crucial mechanism for exercising our spiritual authority. James 5:16 underscores the power of prayer, declaring that the prayer of a righteous person is powerful and effective. Through prayer, we exercise our God-given authority, invoking God's power and will in situations, bringing about change, and impacting our environment and circumstances in line with God's purposes.

With authority also comes great responsibility. We are called to wield our authority judiciously in ways that advance God's kingdom and mirror His character. This responsibility entails making decisions that are grounded in biblical principles, seeking God's guidance, and acting in ways that positively influence those around us and further the cause of Christ.

Walking in authority also means walking in confidence, but this confidence should be tempered with humility, avoiding any form of arrogance. Our confidence is founded on God's power and grace, not our personal abilities or achievements. It is a confidence that acknowledges our dependence on God and recognizes that the authority we wield is a gift from Him to be used for His glory.

So, take a moment to reflect on how you are currently embracing the authority you have as a child of God. Are you using this authority to bring about positive change in your environment? Do your actions and decisions reflect the character and will of God? Embrace your God-given authority with a heart full of humility and responsibility, using it as a tool to fulfill your divine calling and make a lasting impact in the world for God's kingdom.

As we continue to navigate this chapter, let's do so with an awareness of the authority that comes with our sonship. Let's strive to understand this authority, walk in it with humility and wisdom, and use it to honor God and advance His purposes. Let's embrace our authority as children of God, recognizing it as a powerful tool for kingdom work, spiritual growth, and making a meaningful difference in our world. Let's commit to using our authority responsibly, in service to others, and for the glory of God, confident in His power working through us.

LIVING AUTHENTICALLY

In this final section of the chapter, our attention turns to fully embracing and living out our authentic identity as children of God. This final section is not just about acknowledging our status as God's children in belief but about integrating this identity into every facet of our lives, ensuring that our sonship is reflected in our actions, decisions, and relationships.

A genuine, deep relationship with God is at the heart of authentic sonship. This relationship is characterized by honesty and transparency both with God and ourselves. Psalm 139:23-24 exemplifies this, inviting us to ask God to search our hearts and reveal any aspects of our lives that are not aligned with His will. True sonship involves an openness to God's examination and a willingness to adjust our lives according to His guidance.

Authentic sonship also demands consistency between our faith and daily life. It's about ensuring that our decisions, interactions, and relationships reflect our identity in Christ. Colossians 3:17 captures this idea, instructing us to do everything, whether in word or deed, in the name of Jesus. This consistency is a testimony to the authenticity of our faith and a reflection of Christ in us.

Jesus warned against the leaven of the Pharisees, which is hypocrisy (Luke 12:1). As children of God, we must guard against the temptation to live a life of duplicity, where our outward appearance does not match our inner reality. Hypocrisy undermines our witness and hinders our relationship with God and with others.

Embracing vulnerability is a key aspect of walking authentically with God. Acknowledging our weaknesses and struggles, as Paul did in 2 Corinthians 12:9-10, allows God's power to be made perfect in our imperfections. This vulnerability is not a sign of weakness but a testament to the transformative power of God working in and through us.

Reflecting God in our actions is a hallmark of living authentically as His child. The fruit of the Spirit, described in Galatians 5:22-23, should be manifested in our lives, demonstrating the character and nature of God to those around us. Our actions, imbued with love, joy, peace, patience, kindness, goodness, faithfulness, gentleness, and self-control, show the world the transformative impact of a life surrendered to God.

The impact of living authentically is profound. Our genuine faith journey becomes a beacon of hope and encouragement to others. It bears witness to the truth of the Gospel and exemplifies the power of a life changed by God.

As we wrap up this chapter on the truths and responsibilities of sonship, we prepare to transition into Chapter Ten, "Living as a Son - Practical Applications." This next chapter will delve into the practicalities of applying the principles of sonship in everyday life. It will explore how to ensure that our identity as children of God is not just a theological concept but a living reality that influences our decisions, shapes our relationships, and guides our journey.

In conclusion, as we move forward from understanding the sobering truths of sonship to applying them in practical ways, let's do so with a heart committed to authenticity. Let's strive to live out our identity as God's children in every aspect of our lives, reflecting His character and walking in His ways. Let's embrace the fullness of sonship, living authentically and purposefully, allowing our relationship with God to permeate every area of our existence. Let's commit to a life that professes faith in Christ and demonstrates it through our actions, choices, and interactions with others.

CHALLENGES FORTIFY OUR FAITH AND STRENGTHEN OUR CHARACTER.

CHAPTER TEN

LIVING AS A SON

This conversation marks a pivotal shift from understanding our identity as children of God to actively implementing this understanding in our daily lives. This chapter is about translating our faith into tangible actions, ensuring that our identity as God's children is reflected in every aspect of our routine, from the moment we wake up to our interactions at work and home.

Starting each day with God lays a strong foundation for integrating faith into our daily lives. Engaging in morning prayer, meditation on Scripture, or worship helps set the tone for the day ahead. This practice aligns our thoughts and actions with God's will, as highlighted in Psalm 5:3, where the psalmist talks about laying requests before God each morning and waiting in expectation. This daily commitment helps center our focus on God, allowing His guidance to permeate our decisions and interactions throughout the day.

Incorporating faith into our decision-making process is crucial. Our faith should be the lens through which we view and make all our choices, from the seemingly trivial to the life-altering. Proverbs 3:5-6 reminds us of the importance of trusting in the Lord with all our heart and not relying solely on our understanding. Acknowledging God in all our ways ensures that our decisions are good for us and align with His divine plan.

Our workplace is a primary arena where our faith should be evident. Integrating faith into our work goes beyond ethical behavior; it involves demonstrating our faith through our work ethic, interactions with colleagues, and integrity. Colossians 3:23-24 urges us to work heartily, as for the Lord and not for men, reflecting the excellence, commitment, and ethical standards that befit a child of God. Our approach to work, our attitude towards colleagues, and our dedication to our tasks can serve as powerful testimonies of our faith.

Our faith should be a guiding force in our family and relational dynamics. Relationships with family and friends present opportunities to express God's love, forgiveness, and grace. Ephesians 4:2-3 calls us to be humble, gentle, patient, and bear with one another in love, striving to maintain unity. These principles should govern our interactions with those closest to us, shaping our responses and actions in a way that honors God and builds healthy, loving relationships.

Facing challenges and difficulties is an inevitable part of life, but our response to these trials should reflect our faith. James 1:12 assures us of blessings for those who persevere under trial. Confronting challenges with faith, patience, and reliance on God, rather than succumbing to despair or frustration, is a powerful demonstration of the strength and depth of our conviction. It's about trusting God's sovereignty and finding peace and strength in His promises.

Sharing our faith with others is also a critical aspect of living authentically as a child of God. This sharing does not always mean engaging in overt evangelism but can manifest in acts of kindness, offering support, and leading a life that naturally draws others to Christ. Our actions, attitudes, and words can serve as powerful tools in sharing the love and truth of God with those around us.

In this section, take time to reflect on how your faith manifests in your daily activities. Are there areas in your life where your faith could be more evident? Consider ways you can more actively integrate your faith into every part of your day. Whether it's through intentional prayer, making God-centered decisions, demonstrating Christ's love in your relationships, or facing challenges with a godly attitude, each aspect of your day is an opportunity to live out your sonship.

Let's approach each day as an opportunity to demonstrate our identity as children of God. Let's commit to practices that keep us rooted in Him, make decisions that reflect His will, and interact with others in a way that demonstrates His love. Let's embrace the challenge of living out our faith in practical, tangible ways, ensuring that our daily walk is a true reflection of our sonship and a testament to the transformative power of living in Christ.

The Outward Expression of Faith

Let's shift our focus to serving others, which is a vital and outward expression of our faith. Service is not merely an obligation but an authentic manifestation of God's love and grace through our actions. As children of God, we are called to embody His compassion and care for others in tangible ways.

Service as a lifestyle is a key concept in sonship. It extends beyond structured activities or events; it's an integral part of our daily life as Christians. Galatians 5:13 calls us to serve one another humbly in love, highlighting that service is woven into the very fabric of our Christian walk. It's about seeing our everyday life as a continuous opportunity to serve others.

Identifying opportunities to serve requires attentiveness and responsiveness to the needs around us. These opportunities can arise in various contexts - within our families, workplaces, communities, or churches. It's about being observant and ready to act when we see a need, understanding that service is not limited to grand gestures but is often found in the simple acts of kindness and help we can offer every day.

Our unique talents and gifts are given to us for the purpose of serving others. 1 Peter 4:10-11 speaks to this, encouraging us to use our gifts to serve others, thereby administering God's grace in its various forms. This action means recognizing and utilizing our abilities not for self-promotion but for the benefit of others and the glorification of God.

The impact of serving others is profound. It meets physical and emotional needs and can also open hearts to the message of Christ. Our service is a living testimony of our faith and can often speak louder than words. It demonstrates the practical and transformative power of God's love in action.

Service, however, does not always need to be grand or elaborate. Often, simple acts of kindness—offering a listening ear, helping a neighbor, or providing a word of encouragement—can have a significant impact on others. What truly matters is the heart behind the service—the intention to reflect God's love and compassion.

While serving others is important, it's also crucial to maintain a balance and practice self-care. Overextending ourselves can lead to burnout, making it challenging to serve effectively. Self-care ensures that we can continue to serve others joyfully and sustainably.

Reflect on how service is integrated into your daily life. Consider how your actions can serve as an extension of your faith, demonstrating God's love in practical ways to those around you. Think about your unique gifts and how they can be used to serve others. Look for opportunities in your everyday interactions to serve and remember that even the smallest act of kindness can have a significant impact. Let's embrace service as a natural and essential part of our identity as children of God. Let's seek to serve in both big and small ways, using our gifts and talents for the betterment of others and the glory of God. Let's approach service with a heart full of love and humility, balancing our efforts with self-care to ensure that our service is sustainable and joy-filled. Let's live out our faith through service, demonstrating the love of Christ in every interaction and making a tangible difference in the world around us.

USING WHAT WE'RE GIVEN

This section underscores that as sons of God, we are entrusted with various resources—time, talents, finances, and relationships—and how we manage and utilize these gifts significantly reflects our understanding of sonship and our dedication to God's kingdom.

Stewardship is an integral part of our walk with God and should be viewed as an act of worship. When we manage our resources wisely and responsibly, we honor God and recognize that all we have is from Him. 1 Chronicles 29:14 poignantly reminds us that we are merely stewards of God's bounty, and our giving and managing are ways of returning to Him what is inherently His.

Time is one of the most valuable resources God has given us. Ephesians 5:15-16 challenges us to make the most of every opportunity, recognizing the brevity and preciousness of the time we have. This involves prioritizing activities and commitments that align with God's will and purpose, ensuring that our time is used effectively for kingdom purposes.

Our talents and abilities are gifts from God, meant to be used not just for personal achievement but for serving others and bringing glory to God. The parable of the talents in Matthew 25:14-30 is a stark reminder that we must utilize our God-given abilities to their fullest potential, not bury them out of fear or neglect.

Financial stewardship is also a key aspect of our walk with God. How we handle our finances reflects our values and faith. 2 Corinthians 9:6-7 teaches us the importance of giving generously and cheerfully, emphasizing that our attitude towards giving is as important as the act itself. Financial stewardship involves integrity, generosity, and recognizing that our finances are tools for advancing God's work.

Furthermore, stewardship extends to how we nurture our relationships. Colossians 3:12-14 calls us to clothe ourselves with virtues like compassion, kindness, humility, gentleness, and patience. Our relationships should be stewarded with love, forgiveness, and a commitment to reflect Christ's love in our interactions with others.

The impact of godly stewardship is far-reaching. Effective stewardship of our time, talents, finances, and relationships can significantly impact our lives, the lives of those around us, and the church's broader mission. It's about contributing to the advancement of God's kingdom in practical and meaningful ways, reflecting God's generosity and love in our actions.

While reflecting on this section, consider how you are currently stewarding the resources God has entrusted you. Evaluate how your management of time, talents, finances, and relationships aligns with your identity as a child of God. Are these resources being used in ways that honor God and demonstrate your commitment to His kingdom? Embrace stewardship as a vital expression of your faith, an act of worship that reflects God's character and love. Let your stewardship be a testament to your faith, a demonstration of your commitment to God's purposes, and a reflection of the transformative impact of His grace in your life.

Let's approach our resources as opportunities to serve God and others. Let's strive to be faithful stewards, using our time, talents, finances, and relationships in ways that glorify God and further His kingdom. Let's embrace stewardship as a key aspect of our identity as God's children, recognizing that how we manage what He has entrusted to us speaks volumes about our understanding of His grace and generosity. It's about seeing every resource as a gift from God, to be used not for our glory but for His and the benefit of others.

Stewardship is more than a responsibility; it's a privilege. It allows us to participate in God's work tangibly, whether by wisely using our time, creatively employing our talents, generously giving our finances, or lovingly nurturing our relationships. Each of these aspects of stewardship is an opportunity to demonstrate our gratitude to God and to make a positive difference in the world.

Let's approach our stewardship with a sense of purpose and joy, knowing that through our faithful management, we can reflect God's character and have a lasting impact on the world around us. Let's be intentional in how we use our resources, always seeking to align our stewardship with God's will and purpose.

So, take a moment to prayerfully consider the areas of stewardship in your life. Ask God to show you how you can better use your time, talents, finances, and relationships for His glory. Commit to making stewardship a key part of your daily walk with God, using what you've been given to serve Him and others and to advance His kingdom on earth.

Remember that stewardship is not just about managing resources; it's about embodying the values of the Kingdom of God in every aspect of our lives. It's a holistic approach to living that honors God and respects the gifts He has given us. As we journey through "Living as a Son - Practical Applications," let's embrace stewardship as a way of life that deeply reflects our faith and commitment to God's purposes.

Let's recognize that each decision we make in stewardship is an opportunity to testify to our faith. Whether it's in how we allocate our time, invest our talents, spend our finances, or cultivate our relationships, each choice can be an act of worship and an expression of our trust in God's provision and guidance. As we steward our resources, let's also be mindful of the impact our choices have on others and the world. Our stewardship can be a powerful tool for good, influencing our communities and contributing to positive change. By managing our resources wisely and generously, we can be a source of blessing and a light in the world, reflecting the love and generosity of our Heavenly Father.

Let this section be a call to action to live out our sonship in practical, impactful ways. Let's steward our resources with wisdom and generosity, making the most of what God has given us for His glory and the good of others. As we do so, let's trust that God will use our efforts to further His kingdom and enrich our journey of faith.

CONTINUAL TRANSFORMATION

The final section of the chapter places emphasis on nurturing our spiritual growth. This journey of ongoing transformation is a vital element of our sonship, indicative of our continuous evolution into the likeness of Christ. This section delves into the various aspects that facilitate this continual spiritual development.

Firstly, a commitment to personal growth is paramount. Spiritual growth doesn't happen passively; it requires intentional engagement with spiritual disciplines like Scripture study, prayer, and meditation. Romans 12:2 underscores the importance of renewing our minds to transform our understanding and discern

God's will, a process integral to spiritual maturation. The role of community in fostering our growth cannot be overstated. As highlighted in Hebrews 10:24-25, Christian fellowship is crucial for encouragement, accountability, and mutual edification. Being part of a faith community allows us to share experiences, learn from one another, and support each other in our spiritual journeys. This togetherness not only spurs us on towards love and good deeds but also provides a network of support and wisdom that is invaluable for personal growth.

Another crucial aspect is embracing trials as opportunities for growth. James 1:2-4 instructs us to consider trials joyfully because they test our faith and develop perseverance, which leads to spiritual maturity. While often difficult, these challenges are instrumental in shaping our character, deepening our faith, and strengthening our reliance on God.

Seeking wisdom and guidance is vital to our spiritual development. Proverbs 4:7 emphasizes the supreme value of wisdom and encourages us to actively pursue it. In our journey of spiritual growth, seeking wisdom through prayer, study, and seeking counsel from more mature Christians is essential for making balanced and godly decisions.

Living a reflective life aids us significantly in our spiritual growth. It involves regularly evaluating our actions, thoughts, and motivations against the teachings of Scripture and adjusting our lives accordingly. This practice of self-examination and reflection helps us to identify areas where we need to grow and align more closely with God's character.

Being open to the Holy Spirit's leading is fundamental for ongoing transformation. Galatians 5:25 exhorts us to live by the Spirit and follow His guidance. The Holy Spirit plays a critical role in our spiritual growth, leading us into deeper truth, convicting us of sin, and empowering us for godly living. Staying sensitive to His promptings ensures that we are continually growing and being transformed from the inside out.

As we wrap up this chapter on practical applications of living as a son of God, we prepare to transition into the final chapter, "The Universal Call to Sonship." This upcoming chapter will explore the inclusive and universal nature of God's call to sonship, highlighting that this divine identity is available to all, irrespective of cultural, ethnic, or social backgrounds. This final chapter invites us to a deeper understanding of God's family and the expansive nature of His love and grace, beckoning all to embrace this transformative identity.

CHAPTER ELEVEN

A *UNIVERSAL CALL* TO *SONSHIP*

In the final chapter, the first section aptly focuses on understanding and embracing the inclusive nature of God's family. This call to sonship is a divine invitation that transcends cultural, ethnic, and social boundaries, welcoming everyone into a profound relationship with God as His children.

The concept of sonship beyond cultural boundaries is a cornerstone of the Gospel message. Galatians 3:28 profoundly states that in Christ, there is neither Jew nor Greek, slave nor free, male nor female; all are one in Jesus Christ. This powerful scripture encapsulates the all-encompassing nature of God's call, affirming that the Gospel is not confined to any specific group but is available to all, regardless of their cultural or ethnic background. This inclusivity is a radical departure from the divisions and hierarchies that often characterize human societies and is a testament to the unifying power of Christ. The global scope of the Gospel is further underscored by the Great Commission in Matthew 28:19-20. Here, Jesus instructs His followers to make disciples of all nations, indicating that the message of salvation and the invitation to sonship are intended for every corner of the earth. This universal outreach reflects God's heart for all humanity and His desire for every person to experience the transformative relationship of being His child.

The role of the church in reflecting this diversity is crucial. As a global family, the church is called to be a microcosm of God's kingdom, embracing and celebrating believers from diverse backgrounds. This diversity within the church is not just about representation; it's about embodying the inclusive nature of God's kingdom and showcasing the unity that can exist among people of different races, cultures, and socioeconomic statuses.

However, achieving true inclusivity in the church can be challenging. Barriers based on race, culture, socioeconomic status, and other factors can hinder the full realization of this divine vision for inclusivity. It's essential for the church to actively work towards breaking down these barriers, fostering an environment where all feel welcomed and valued and where everyone celebrates the diversity of God's family.

Embracing our identity as God's diverse children involves recognizing and celebrating the richness that each unique background brings to the family of believers. It's about understanding that our differences do not divide us but rather enrich our collective experience and understanding of God. This diversity within God's family is a beautiful reflection of His creativity and love for variety.

The impact of inclusive sonship on our witness to the world is profound. When the church truly embodies the diversity and inclusivity of the Gospel, it stands as a powerful testimony to the unifying and transformative power of God's love. It demonstrates that the Gospel transcends human divisions and prejudices, offering a vision of a unified family under God's parenthood.

In your reflection, consider how you and your church community can better mirror the diversity and inclusivity of God's kingdom. Think about ways to embrace and celebrate the variety of backgrounds and experiences within the family of believers. Recognize the value and richness that diversity brings to our understanding of God and our experience as His children.

As we delve into understanding the inclusivity of God's family in this chapter, let's commit to embracing the universal nature of God's call to sonship. Let's work towards creating communities that reflect the diversity of God's kingdom, celebrating our differences and uniting in our shared identity as children of God. Let's allow this understanding of inclusive sonship to shape our interactions, our church communities, and our approach to the world, demonstrating the unifying and inclusive love of God for all humanity.

UNITY IN DIVERSITY

This section emphasizes embracing our collective identity as children of God and celebrating the unity we share in Christ amidst our diversity. It delves into how our diversity, far from being a point of division, enriches our collective experience and strengthens our unity as believers.

The biblical basis for unity among believers is deeply rooted in Scripture. Ephesians 4:4-6 eloquently states that there is one body and one Spirit, just as we are called to one hope, one Lord, one faith, one baptism, and one God and Father of all. This passage underscores the fundamental unity that exists among all believers, regardless of our varied backgrounds, cultures, or experiences. It reminds us that in Christ, our diverse identities converge into a singular, unified body of believers.

Valuing each member's uniqueness is essential to understanding and celebrating this unity. 1 Corinthians 12:12-27 compares the church to a body with many different parts, each with its unique function and importance. This analogy highlights that diversity within the church is not only natural but also necessary for the body of Christ to function effectively. Each believer's unique perspectives, talents, and experiences contribute to the strength and richness of the church.

Overcoming division and fostering unity requires a foundation of love. Colossians 3:14 teaches us to put on love, which binds everything together in perfect harmony. Love is the key to appreciating and respecting our differences while maintaining unity in our faith and purpose. It allows us to see past our individual distinctions and focus on the common bond we share in Christ.

The church plays a crucial role in fostering unity amidst diversity. It should be a place where every believer feels valued and where diversity is celebrated, reflecting the multifaceted nature of God's kingdom. This role involves creating an environment of inclusivity and respect, where differences are tolerated, embraced, and seen as a reflection of God's creativity and love.

Practically, fostering unity involves intentional efforts such as promoting inclusive worship practices, encouraging diverse leadership, and facilitating cross-cultural fellowship. It's about creating spaces within the church where all voices are heard and respected and where every member feels a sense of belonging and contribution, regardless of their background.

Our unity in diversity is a powerful witness to the world. Jesus' prayer in John 17:21-23 for all believers to be one illustrates that our unity is a testament to the reconciling power of the Gospel. It demonstrates to the world the transformative and unifying power of God's love, transcending human divisions and barriers.

Now, take a moment and reflect on how you can contribute to fostering unity within the diverse body of Christ. Think about the steps you and your church community can take to celebrate and embrace diversity, showcasing the universal and inclusive nature of God's call to sonship. Consider how your actions and attitudes can reflect the unity we have in Christ and how you can be an active part of creating a church community that truly mirrors the diversity and unity of God's kingdom.

Embracing our collective identity as children of God involves celebrating our unity in diversity. It's about recognizing that our different backgrounds, cultures, and experiences enrich our shared experience as believers. Let's commit to fostering unity in diversity, both in our individual lives and within our church communities, reflecting the inclusive and unifying love of Christ in all we do.

SONSHIP WITHOUT BORDERS

Our identity compels us to extend our reach and impact beyond our local communities, engaging with the world at large in meaningful and transformative ways. Understanding the global nature of the Gospel is foundational to this endeavor. The Gospel, as emphasized in Mark 16:15, is not limited by geographic or cultural boundaries. Jesus' command to go into all the world and preach the Gospel to every creature underlines the expansive scope of our Christian mission. This global perspective is integral to our understanding of sonship, reminding us that our calling is not just local but universal. Embracing a heart for the nations is a critical step in aligning ourselves with God's global mission.

This act involves developing a genuine concern and love for people from diverse backgrounds and nations, reflecting God's heart for the world as declared in John 3:16. Nurturing this global perspective requires us to look beyond our immediate surroundings and empathize with the joys and struggles of people worldwide.

Engaging globally can take various practical forms. This action may include supporting missionaries financially and through prayer, participating in short-term mission trips, getting involved in global justice issues, or engaging in intercessory prayer for different nations and peoples. Each action represents a tangible expression of our commitment to God's global plan.

The advent of modern technology has significantly enhanced our ability to engage with the world. Social media, online platforms, and digital communication tools have opened new avenues for connecting with individuals and communities across the globe. These technologies enable us to encourage, educate, and share the Gospel with people far beyond our physical reach.

Effective global engagement also requires a deep level of cultural sensitivity and awareness. Understanding and respecting diverse cultural contexts is crucial when sharing the Gospel and engaging in missions. It involves adapting our approach to be culturally appropriate and sensitive, ensuring that our message is conveyed in a way that is respectful and understandable. Local churches play a crucial role in global missions. They serve as launchpads for missionary endeavors, providing training, support, and resources for those called to serve in different parts of the world. Churches can foster a culture of global missions by encouraging their members to participate in and support missionary efforts and ensuring continuous prayer support for missions.

Consider how you can actively participate in God's global mission. Think about ways you can develop a heart for the nations and use your unique resources, skills, and the advantages of technology to make a positive impact globally. Reflect on the steps you can take, both individually and as part of your local church, to contribute to the spread of the Gospel and the fulfillment of God's plan across the world.

Embracing our role in God's global plan is essential to our sonship. It's about understanding and engaging with the world beyond our immediate context, recognizing that our call as children of God is to be a light to all nations. Let's commit to expanding our reach, embracing our global identity, and actively participating in God's mission to bring His love and truth to every corner of the earth.

ANSWERING THE CALL

As we near the conclusion of Chapter 11, we are invited to reflect on the practical steps we can take to truly embrace and live out our identity as sons of God. This journey from understanding to action is a transformative process that reshapes how we view ourselves and our relationship with the divine.

The journey begins with an acknowledgment of the call to sonship. This acknowledgment is more than an intellectual agreement; it's a deep, heartfelt acceptance that God invites every person into a relationship with Him as His child. John 1:12-13 speaks of the right to become children of God, given to those who believe in His name. This acknowledgment is a profound realization that changes our self-perception and deepens our connection with God. It's a recognition that we are loved, valued, and called by God, not as distant beings but as cherished children.

Embracing sonship also requires repentance and acceptance of Christ's salvation. This foundational step is about turning away from our old lives and embracing a new life in Christ. Acts 2:38 emphasizes the importance of repentance and baptism as expressions of accepting Christ's work on the cross for the forgiveness of our sins. This step signifies a profound transformation—a rebirth into a new identity grounded in Christ.

Growth in sonship involves immersing ourselves in the Bible, God's Word. The Scriptures are not just ancient texts but living words that guide, teach, and shape us. 2 Timothy 3:16-17 highlights the critical role of Scripture in teaching, rebuking, correcting, and training in righteousness. Regular engagement with the Bible deepens our understanding of God's character, His desires for our lives, and His plan for humanity. It becomes the lens through which we view the world and our place in it, steadily molding us into more faithful reflections of Christ. Active participation in a Christian community is crucial for nurturing our sonship. Hebrews 10:24-25 encourages believers not to forsake gathering together but to encourage one another. The Christian community provides a space for support, accountability, and spiritual growth. Within this fellowship, we can share our journeys, learn from each other's experiences, and grow in our faith together. The community acts as both a sanctuary and a place of challenge, where we are reminded of our shared identity in Christ and are spurred on to live out this truth.

Cultivating a consistent prayer life is essential in embracing sonship. Philippians 4:6-7 talks about bringing our requests to God with thanksgiving, highlighting prayer as our direct communication line with the divine. In prayer, we not only present our needs and desires but also listen for God's guidance and wisdom. It's a practice that fosters a deeper, more intimate relationship with God, where we can come to understand His will for our lives and find peace and strength in His presence.

Living out our faith in action is a vital aspect of sonship. James 2:17 reminds us that faith without deeds is dead. Our calling as God's children is not to be passive believers but active doers of the Word. This act involves serving others, sharing the Gospel, and applying God's principles in our lives daily. Through these actions, our faith becomes visible, tangible, and impactful, not just for our personal spiritual growth but also for the betterment of the world around us.

Finally, embracing sonship is an ongoing journey of growth and transformation. Romans 12:2 urges us to be transformed by the renewing of our minds. This continual growth involves constantly seeking to align our thoughts, actions, and desires more closely with God's. It's a lifelong process of becoming more like Christ, where each step forward takes us deeper into the heart of God and further into our true identity as His children.

As we conclude this chapter and the book, reflect on your personal journey in embracing sonship. Consider the steps you can take to answer this call more fully. Remember, the journey of sonship is a lifelong process of growth, learning, and transformation, where we are continually called to become more like Christ. Each step on this journey is an opportunity to deepen our relationship with God, to reflect His love and grace more fully in our lives, and to impact the world around us with the truth and beauty of the Gospel. Let us embrace this calling with commitment, joy, and anticipation for all that God has in store for us as His beloved children.

A SON'S REFLECTION

As *Unto Us a Son Is Given* draws to a close, we pause to reflect on the profound journey of understanding and embracing our divine legacy as sons of God. This journey, a lifelong quest of discovery and growth, has taken us through the multifaceted aspects of what it means to be called to sonship—a calling steeped in responsibility, service, stewardship, and profound transformation in Christ. Central to our exploration has been the universal nature of God's call to sonship. This call breaks through all human-made barriers, extending a transformative invitation to every individual, regardless of background, culture, or past. It stands as an open invitation, echoing God's inclusive heart and welcoming all into a relationship that redefines identity and purpose.

Embracing sonship goes beyond intellectual understanding. It's a call to live out our identity in Christ every day. Living out the call involves more than just personal piety; it's about integrating our faith into every facet of our existence. It's serving others with a love that mirrors Christ's, stewarding the resources God has entrusted to us wisely, and committing ourselves to continual growth in spiritual maturity.

Throughout this journey, the role of community has been undeniably significant. Fellowship with other believers profoundly enriches and supports our walk as children of God. The church isn't just a gathering; it's a nurturing ground, a place of guidance, and a supportive family that walks alongside us as we pursue this divine calling.

This book is more than just a collection of concepts and principles; it's a call to action. It's an invitation to step into the fullness of our identity as God's children. It encourages us to embrace this identity and actively live it out in service, love, and unwavering commitment to the advancement of God's kingdom.

So, let us look forward with hope and anticipation to the continuing journey ahead. The path of sonship is one of endless discovery, offering continuous opportunities for growth and boundless joy in the Lord. It's a path that calls for faith, perseverance, and a deepening love for our Heavenly Father.

Let this book encourage you to embrace your divine destiny as a child of God. Let your life be a living testament to His love and grace. Step forward in faith, knowing that you are an integral part of God's grand narrative of redemption and love—a narrative in which each of us has a significant role to play. May we walk this path with hearts open to God's leading, hands ready to serve, and spirits willing to be transformed into the likeness of Christ. As we do so, may we find that in embracing our sonship, we discover not only our true selves but also the heart of God and the richness of His love for us.

Let us carry this understanding into every aspect of our lives, allowing it to shape our actions, guide our decisions, and influence our interactions with others. This journey of sonship is not just about what we receive as children of God but also about what we give back to the world around us. It's about reflecting God's love in our communities, being His hands and feet in a world that desperately needs His touch. As we walk this path, let us be mindful of the impact we can have, the lives we can touch, and the difference we can make when we fully embrace our identity as God's children.

In conclusion, *Unto Us a Son Is Given* is more than just a book; it's a roadmap for a life transformed by the profound reality of being a son of God. As you move forward, carry the lessons and truths you have learned here into your daily life. Let them guide you as you continue to grow, serve, and live out the extraordinary calling God has placed upon your life. Embrace this journey with passion and purpose, and step into the incredible destiny God has for you as His beloved child.

ABOUT THE AUTHOR

Kyren J. Garel is a visionary leader, dedicated mentor, and passionate minister with a profound commitment to faith, technology, and community empowerment. Holding a Bachelor of Business Administration from Jackson State University and currently pursuing an MBA at the University of Arizona, Kyren has built a robust career at Microsoft. As a seasoned Cloud Solution Architect with a Top Secret clearance and a PROSCI Change Practitioner certification, he has made significant strides in advancing cloud adoption and driving organizational transformation.

Kyren's journey is marked by a relentless pursuit of excellence, evident in his innovative problem-solving and strategic leadership. Beyond his corporate achievements, he is the founder of King's Academy, a mentorship organization dedicated to empowering men and fostering their spiritual growth and development. As a worship leader and licensed minister, Kyren's ministry is dedicated to helping God's people discover, understand, and unapologetically live out their God-given purpose.

In *Unto Us a Son Is Given*, Kyren Garel draws upon his diverse experiences and deep spiritual insights to illuminate the transformational power of sonship. This book is a heartfelt exploration of faith, hope, and divine purpose, guiding readers from the bondage of an orphan spirit to the liberating embrace of spiritual adoption. Through a unique blend of business acumen, spiritual leadership, and heartfelt storytelling, Kyren offers a compelling guide to understanding our true identity in Christ and navigating life's challenges with unwavering faith and boldness. At its heart, this book is a powerful invitation to embrace the fullness of our calling, stepping confidently into our roles as beloved children of God and reflecting His love and grace in a world in need.

CONNECT WITH KYREN

INSTAGRAM	@KyrenGarel
YOUTUBE	Kyren Garel
LINKEDIN	Kyren Garel
EMAIL	info@garelglobal.com

Milton Keynes UK
Ingram Content Group UK Ltd.
UKHW030145051224
452010UK00001B/125